America and the World:
A Diplomatic History
Part I

Professor Mark A. Stoler

THE TEACHING COMPANY ®

PUBLISHED BY:

THE TEACHING COMPANY
4151 Lafayette Center Drive, Suite 100
Chantilly, Virginia 20151-1232
1-800-TEACH-12
Fax—703-378-3819
www.teach12.com

ISBN 1-59803-476-6

Mark A. Stoler, Ph.D.

Professor Emeritus of History, The University of Vermont

Mark A. Stoler is a Professor Emeritus of History at The University of Vermont, where he specialized from 1970 to 2007 in U.S. diplomatic and military history. He received his B.A. from the City College of New York and his M.A. and Ph.D. from the University of Wisconsin–Madison.

Professor Stoler is the author of *The Politics of the Second Front: American Military Planning and Diplomacy in Coalition Warfare, 1941–1943* (Greenwood, 1977); *Explorations in American History*, with Marshall True (Knopf, 1986); *George C. Marshall: Soldier-Statesman of the American Century* (Twayne, 1989); *Allies and Adversaries: The Joint Chiefs of Staff, the Grand Alliance, and U.S. Strategy in World War II* (University of North Carolina Press, 2000); *Debating Franklin D. Roosevelt's Foreign Policies, 1933–1945*, with Justus Doenecke (Rowman and Littlefield, 2005); *Allies in War: Britain and America Against the Axis Powers, 1940–1945* (Hodder-Arnold, 2005); and numerous articles and book chapters on U.S. diplomatic and military history. Professor Stoler is also the editor of *The Origins of the Cold War* (Scholarly Resources, 1981) and *Major Problems in the History of World War II*, with Melanie Gustafson (Houghton Mifflin, 2003).

Professor Stoler has been a visiting professor at the U.S. Naval War College (1980–1981), Fulbright Professor at the University of Haifa in Israel (1984–1985), visiting Professor at the U.S. Military Academy at West Point (1994–1995), the Harold K. Johnson Visiting Professor at the U.S. Army Military History Institute (2004–2005), and the Stanley Kaplan Distinguished Visiting Professor of American Foreign Policy at Williams College (2007–2008).

His multiple awards include the Distinguished Book Award of the Society for Military History for *Allies and Adversaries*; inclusion in *Who's Who Among America's Teachers*; The University of Vermont's Kidder Outstanding Faculty Award, University Scholar Award, Dean's Lecture Award, and Kroepsch-Maurice Excellence in Teaching Award; honorary membership in the university's chapter of Phi Beta Kappa; and two public service awards from the U.S. Army.

Professor Stoler is a member of the Board of Trustees of the Society for Military History and the Presidential Counselors Advisory Body of the National World War II Museum and has previously served on the Army's Historical Advisory Committee, the Board of Directors of the World War II Studies Association, and the Council of the Society for Historians of American Foreign Relations. He was the 2004 president of that society.

Table of Contents
America and the World: A Diplomatic History
Part I

America and the World: A Diplomatic History

Scope:

Today, the United States ranks as the most powerful and influential nation not only in the contemporary world but in all of world history. In both relative and absolute terms, its power and influence are totally unprecedented. Not since the heyday of the Roman Empire has any single nation even approached such an extraordinary position.

That was not always the case. Indeed, in 1776, the United States consisted of 13 weak and sparsely settled colonies that appeared utterly incapable even of maintaining their just-declared independence, let alone achieving great-power status. Even after they succeeded in obtaining British recognition of their independence, the states still constituted one of the weakest countries in the world—one that barely survived on the periphery of international politics.

How, then, did the United States shift from such weakness and peripheral status to its current position of unprecedented global power and influence? This course explores how and why the nation was able to do so between 1776 and 1991 by examining some of the key events, ideas, and personalities in the history of U.S. foreign relations.

We will first examine the colonial and revolutionary origins of the key beliefs that Americans developed, many of which they still hold today, about international relations and their role in the world. We will also look at how they managed to defeat Great Britain, the greatest empire in the world at that time, and how they managed to defend their independence from 1783–1815 against a still-hostile Britain, as well as a host of other hostile powers. In the process, we will explore the Constitution as a foreign policy document and the domestic debate in the late 18th and early 19th centuries between the followers of Thomas Jefferson and those of Alexander Hamilton regarding the proper foreign policy for the young nation to pursue. Within that debate, you will be introduced to some of the key documents and events in the early history of American foreign relations: Jay's Treaty, Washington's Farewell Address, the XYZ Affair and the Quasi War with France, the Louisiana Purchase, and the War of 1812.

With the end of that war in 1814–1815, the United States was able to turn its attention away from Europe and toward continued westward expansion across the North American continent. The next section of the course will explore this process, with special emphasis on the expansionist ideology known as Manifest Destiny; key policymakers, such as John Quincy Adams and James K. Polk; and such pivotal documents and events as the 1819 Transcontinental Treaty, the Monroe Doctrine, the war with Mexico, and the acquisition of Texas, California, New Mexico, and Oregon. By 1848, the United States had, as a result of these acquisitions, become one of the largest countries in the world, stretching across the entire North American continent from the Atlantic to the Pacific. This enormous expansion dramatically exacerbated sectional tensions, however, leading to a temporary end to further territorial expansion and to a civil war that almost destroyed the nation between 1861 and 1865. The failure of Europe to intervene on the side of the South was pivotal to Union victory and the continued rise of American power, and it is analyzed in the concluding lecture to this section of the course.

The next section explores the full emergence of the United States as one of the world's great powers that occurred in the late 19th and early 20th centuries. The major source for this new status was the Industrial Revolution that, by the 1890s, had transformed the United States into the greatest economic power in the world. Along with that economic power came a war with Spain in 1898 and a new burst of territorial expansion, this time, primarily through the acquisition of overseas colonies in the Caribbean and the Pacific rather than contiguous land in North America. Simultaneously, the United States used its enormous economic power to create an informal empire in Latin America.

From 1914–1918 and again from 1939–1945, Europe plunged into two world wars. Despite a stated desire to refrain from participation in either war and, thus, retain its isolationist tradition vis-à-vis Europe, the United States wound up as an active participant in both conflicts. This section of the course explores how and why the United States entered each world war and its role in each Allied victory. It also explores Washington's subsequent emergence, by 1945, as the world's greatest diplomatic, military, and economic power, with commentators referring to the country as a superpower.

The United States was not, however, the only superpower in the world in 1945. Its Russian ally had also emerged from World War II with enormously expanded power and influence, and within a short period of time, the two nations shifted from wartime allies to global adversaries. Indeed, from 1945 to 1991, they waged a global Cold War that consistently threatened to turn into a third world war. It did not do so, though the United States did fight two limited but bloody wars in the context of the Cold War, one in Korea and the other in Vietnam. This last section of the course examines these specific wars, as well as the overarching Cold War and the eventual American victory in that conflict.

Victory in the Cold War removed what appeared to be the only remaining threat to American global hegemony. Indeed, by 1991, the United States had defeated not only every nation that had threatened its global dominance but, in the process, every competing ideology: first, monarchism; then, fascism/Nazism; and finally, Communism. Some commentators consequently spoke of an "end of history" in an ideological sense, with American democratic capitalism in the form of globalization sweeping the world. But then came 9/11 and the global conflict that we live with today.

As we will see at the end of the course, the roots of this conflict may be traced to our own arrogance, and perhaps one of the lessons we can learn from it is to seek, in the words of Reinhold Niebuhr, "the serenity to accept the things we cannot change, the courage to change the things we can, and the wisdom to know the difference."

Lecture One
Achieving Independence

Scope:

Isolationism, mission, expansionism, idealism, and realism are but a few of the many terms used to describe the central themes in the history of U.S. foreign relations. This lecture explores the origins of these themes in early American history and their importance in America's eventual rise to superpower status. It also examines their apparent contradictions, especially as they emerged during the Revolutionary War.

Most notable in this regard was the conflict between the republican ideology Americans espoused and the realities they faced in achieving independence from Great Britain. The former placed them at odds with every monarchy in Europe, whereas the latter required alliance with, and military assistance from, those very monarchies, particularly the French, whom they had fought against in numerous wars throughout the century. This lecture examines how and why the Americans were able to obtain French assistance and the resulting shift of the Revolutionary War to a world war that forced the British to accept American independence. In the process, we will explore the dichotomy between idealistic statements by the American revolutionaries and their very realistic diplomacy within the European monarchial system.

Outline

I.   This course explores how and why the United States transformed itself from an initial position of weakness to its current status as a superpower. Our primary approach will be a chronological examination of key events, ideas, and personalities in the history of U.S. foreign relations. We begin by going back to 1776 and even earlier to explore the origins of some of the major beliefs and themes that will reappear throughout the course.

II. In the process of declaring their independence in 1776, Americans enunciated a series of beliefs about international relations and their place in the world. These beliefs would become central themes in the rise to superpower status.

A. Some of these beliefs constitute what historians label the "idealistic" strand in American foreign relations. The basic concepts in this strand are as follows:

   1. America was both geographically and ideologically distinct from Europe, its monarchial system of government, and its ensuing wars.

   2. America could and should maintain a policy of isolationism vis-à-vis those European wars and should be able to use trade as means of detaching itself from European conflict.

   3. Simultaneously, America was to be the global haven of liberty, with a mission to spread such liberty to Europe and, thus, to help overthrow the monarchial system that tyrannized the peoples of Europe and caused widespread war.

   4. Americans were also destined to expand across the North American continent and establish what Thomas Jefferson would later call "an empire of liberty."

B. All these ideas originated long before 1776 and had deep roots in both European and American colonial history.

   1. Isolationism and geographic distinction are both part of the same concept that Europeans had long accepted: the idea that the Western Hemisphere constituted a separate world and that war or peace in one world did not necessarily mean war or peace in the other.

   2. The movement from England to North America was itself an act of isolationism. Many colonists desired to escape the problems of the Old World and start fresh in the New World.

   3. The unique American "mission" similarly has its origins in early colonial history. The early Puritans left England for Massachusetts Bay to escape problems in England, notably religious persecution, and establish a model Christian community to reform the corrupt Church of England.

   4. The very act of colonizing the New World was a form of imperial expansion, supported by the English government as a way of expanding the British Empire.

C. In 1776, these ideas were restated in new form, most clearly by Thomas Paine (1737–1809) in his famous pamphlet *Common Sense*.

    1. But to defeat Great Britain, Americans would need recognition and military assistance from the very European monarchies they wished to destroy, particularly the French, with whom they had fought four bloody wars since 1689.

    2. To obtain that help, American leaders relied on a tradition of realism far divorced from the idealistic statements in *Common Sense*.

D. That realistic tradition also had deep roots in colonial history. For nearly two centuries, the colonists had been part of the European system of alliances, wars, and empires and had, thus, learned the rules of mercantilism and realpolitik that European nations practiced. The most important of these rules revolved around three core principles:

    1. The best way to obtain, maintain, and organize national wealth is to create a self-sufficient empire and a favorable balance of trade with other empires.

    2. In a capitalist system, wealth can create wealth, which means that wealth is essentially infinite. In a mercantile system, however, the wealth of the world is finite. The only way to gain wealth is to take it away from another nation, usually by war, or else it will be taken from one's own nation.

    3. All other nations are, therefore, potential threats. The core principle to keep in mind is that the present enemy of our present enemy is our temporary friend and ally.

III. These beliefs firmly guided American leaders during the War for Independence and established a tradition of realism in foreign policy to balance the idealism being simultaneously expressed.

A. America's first great successes in foreign policy came in 1778 with the Treaty of Commerce and the Treaty of Alliance with France. Benjamin Franklin (1706–1790) and his colleagues negotiated these agreements with the French foreign minister, Charles Gravier, comte de Vergennes, after the great American military victory at Saratoga.

1. French military assistance proved critical to the American war effort, especially at the decisive Yorktown campaign.
2. French diplomacy brought Spain and other European nations into the conflict as either allies of France or friendly neutrals, though not as formal allies of the United States.

B. As a result, Britain found itself in a world war and diplomatically isolated by 1781. After Yorktown, the English decided to make peace with the Americans as a means of dividing their enemies and minimizing their losses.

C. In the ensuing peace negotiations, the Americans once again practiced realpolitik, violating the spirit if not the letter of the French alliance by conducting separate negotiations with, and obtaining highly favorable terms from, the British.

D. Yet in their ensuing euphoria, Americans tended to ignore these facts and see their success in idealistic terms, as divinely inspired and destined to result in the remaking of the entire world. Such beliefs would have a major impact on the future behavior of Americans.

Suggested Readings:

Dull, *A Diplomatic History of the American Revolution.*

Gilbert, *To the Farewell Address*, chs. 1–4.

Savelle with Fisher, *The Origins of American Diplomacy.*

Questions to Consider:

1. How and why did 17th- and 18th-century Americans develop a unique view of themselves and their place in international relations?

2. What diplomatic and military factors accounted for American success in the War for Independence?

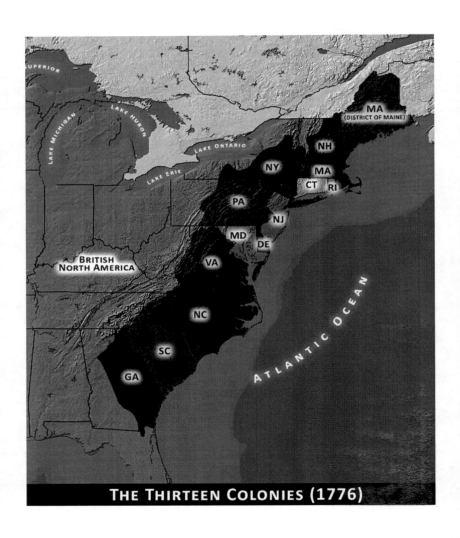

THE THIRTEEN COLONIES (1776)

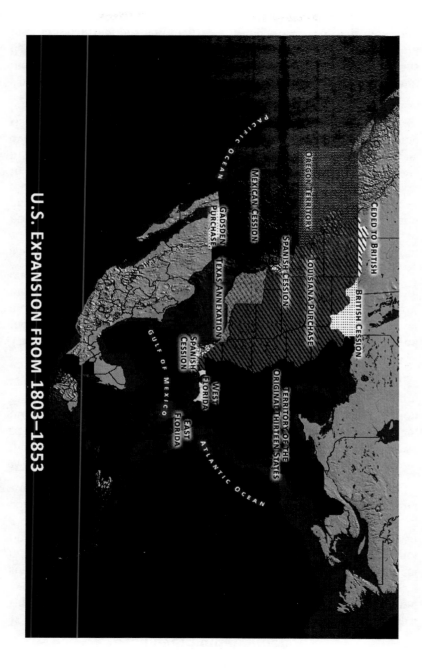

U.S. EXPANSION FROM 1803–1853

Lecture One—Transcript
Achieving Independence

Welcome to this course on the birth and rise of the United States as a superpower. The term "superpower" was first coined in 1944, and ever since, it has had numerous definitions. Some define a superpower as a nation able to project its power globally. Others get much more specific and say it must include the ability to project not only military power but also economic, political, and social power globally. And by some definitions, that in turn, requires a continental-size landmass, a large population, a nuclear capacity, and a universal ideology.

Whichever definition one chooses, the United States has, for more than half a century, been one of the superpowers. Since the collapse of the Soviet Union in 1991, it has been the only superpower. Indeed, the United States is not only the most powerful and influential nation in the world, [but] it is also the most powerful and influential nation the world has ever seen. Not since the heyday of the Roman Empire has any nation even approached such an extraordinary position.

That was not always the case. In 1776, the United States appeared incapable even of maintaining its just-declared independence, let alone achieving superpower status. Even after winning its war for independence, it remained one of the weakest countries in the world, one that barely survived on the periphery of international politics.

This course will explore how and why the United States shifted from such weakness to its present superpower position. It will do so primarily via a chronological examination of key events, ideas, and personalities in the history of U.S. foreign relations, a history I have taught for many years at the University of Vermont and elsewhere. In the process, the course will also deal with some of the numerous historical disagreements that exist regarding many of these ideas, events, and personalities, and it will analyze key documents in the rise of American power within the context of their times, as well as later and different meanings.

The first section of the course, running from the colonial era through the War of 1812, will examine the origins of key beliefs Americans developed—many of which they still hold today—about international relations and their role in the world. We will then look at how they managed to defeat Great Britain, the greatest empire in the world, and to defend their independence from 1776 to 1815 against not only Great Britain but a host of hostile European powers. In the process, we will explore the Revolutionary War diplomacy, then the Constitution as a foreign policy document, and then the huge partisan debate that followed between the followers of Alexander Hamilton and Thomas Jefferson regarding the proper foreign policy for the young nation to pursue.

In the next (second) section of the course, our attention will shift from survival amidst European threats to the enormous expansion of U.S. size and power that occurred in the century following the War of 1812. First, [we will look at] territorial expansion across the continent that occurred from 1815 to 1848 and made the United States one of the largest nations in the world. Then, [we'll turn to] the resulting sectional crisis and Civil War that brought the era of continental expansion to an end and almost destroyed the nation. In particular, we will look at Union diplomacy during this time that prevented a decisive European intervention on the side of the South. We will then look at the full emergence of the United States as one of the world's great powers after the Civil War as a result, first, of its enormous Industrial Revolution and, then, its translation of its new economic power into political and military power during and after the 1898 war with Spain and the accompanying burst of overseas territorial expansion in the Caribbean and the Pacific. Of equal if not more importance, we will also explore American use of its enormous economic power to create an informal empire during this time period.

Then, in the third section of the course, we will look at the years 1914 to 1945, during which the United States entered two World Wars of European origins, despite a stated desire to retain its traditional isolation from such European conflicts. We will then explore how and why this intervention occurred, the American role in each Allied victory, and the nation's subsequent emergence by 1945 with superpower status as the world's greatest diplomatic and military power, as well as the world's greatest economic power.

In the fourth section, we will focus on the years 1945 to 1991 and the global Cold War that occurred between the United States and the other nation to emerge from World War II with superpower status, the Soviet Union. That Cold War consistently threatened to turn into a third world war, and it did lead to two limited but bloody wars for the United States within the Cold War, Korea and Vietnam. This last section of the course explores these specific wars, as well as the overarching Cold War and the eventual American victory in that Cold War.

The American victory in the Cold War removed what appeared to be the only remaining threat to U.S. global hegemony, but then came 9/11 and the conflict that we live with today. The final lecture in this course summarizes the reasons for America's rise and status as the sole superpower, as well as the ensuing search over the last decade and a half for an appropriate global policy in light of world conditions. But let us start by going back to 1776 and even earlier to explore the origins of some of the major beliefs and themes that will reappear throughout this entire course.

In the process of declaring independence in 1776, Americans enunciated a series of beliefs about international relations and their place in the world which would become central themes in their rise to superpower status. Some of these constitute what historians label the "idealistic" strand in American foreign relations.

What are these beliefs? [First,] that America was ideologically as well as geographically distinct from Europe, its monarchial system of government, and its ensuing wars. Second, that America could and should isolate itself from those European wars and that it would be able to use its trade as a means of doing so. Thirdly, America was to be the global haven of liberty, with a mission to spread such liberty to Europe and, thus, to help overthrow the tyrannical monarchial system that supposedly caused all of these wars. Americans also viewed themselves as destined to expand across the North American continent and establish what Thomas Jefferson would later call "an empire of liberty."

All of these ideas originated long before 1776 and had deep roots in both European history and American colonial history. Isolationism and geographic distinction were both parts of a concept that Europeans as well as American colonists had long accepted: that the Western Hemisphere constituted a separate world and that war or peace in one world might not necessarily mean war or peace in the other world. Furthermore, the movement from England to North America was itself an act of isolation for many colonists who desired to escape the problems of the Old World and begin anew in this New World.

The concept of a unique American "mission" similarly had its origins in early colonial history. Indeed, early 17th-century Puritans left England for Massachusetts Bay in order not only to escape their problems in England (most notably but not exclusively religious persecution) but also to establish in the New World a model Christian community to reform the corrupt Church of England and, eventually, other corrupt churches. As their leader John Winthrop put it: "We shall be as a city upon a hill; the eyes of all people are upon us." The very act of colonizing the New World was also an act of imperial expansion supported by the English government as a way of expanding the British Empire.

In 1776, all of these ideas would be restated in new form, most clearly by Thomas Paine in his famous pamphlet *Common Sense*. *Common Sense* is known as a propaganda pamphlet designed to get the colonists to support complete independence from England, but it is also a key foreign policy document, with foreign policy arguments used to get the colonists to support independence. How? Paine argued that the colonists did not need British military protection, that indeed, the colonial connection with England and its monarchial system of government had been the cause of involvement in European wars. As Paine put it: "France and Spain never were, nor perhaps ever will be, our enemies as Americans, but as our being the subjects of Great Britain." Paine also argued that colonial commerce, especially in the foodstuffs that we produce, would ensure us peaceful relations with the nations of Europe; as he put it: "while eating is the custom of Europe … [o]ur plan is commerce," Paine continued, "and that, well attended to, will secure us the peace and friendship of all Europe because it is in the interest of Europe to have America as a free port." Given these facts, the colonists should "form no partial [that is, political] connection with any part of Europe." Paine continued: "This new world," as he put it, "has been and shall remain the asylum for the persecuted lovers of civil and religious liberty from every part of Europe. … The birthday of a new world is at hand." And this asylum of liberty, Paine went on, shall expand. Throughout *Common Sense*, there are constant references to the absurdity of England as an island governing an entire continent. Implicitly, Paine was stating that the colonists would expand across the entire continent.

To defeat Great Britain, Americans would need the recognition and the military assistance of the very European monarchies they wished to destroy—most notably, the French, with whom they had fought four bloody wars since 1689. To obtain that help, American leaders relied upon a tradition of realism far divorced from the idealistic statements in *Common Sense*. That realistic tradition also had deep roots in colonial history, as the colonists had, for nearly two centuries, actually been part of the European system of alliances, wars, and empires and had, thus, learned the rules of realpolitik and of mercantilism that European nations practiced at this time.

Realpolitik was an old European tradition. Essentially, it argued that the basic interest of all states was security in an anarchic world and, thus, the acquisition of power and of wealth. Morality was irrelevant in such a world and, perhaps, even immoral. For example, what if you were the ruler of a nation who insisted on operating on a proper, individual moral code of honesty, but all other rulers lied and cheated and were immoral? In practicing your morality, you would be putting your nation at risk, the security of your people at risk. Your prime reason for being a ruler—the prime directive, if you will—was the protection of your people, so by thus acting morally, you would be behaving immorally.

If you follow this line of thought, you have a basic ensuing principle: Every other nation in the world is a potential threat. Remember, all nations claim sovereignty, and that includes the right to make war on other nations. So all nations are potential threats, and the present enemy of my present enemy is, thus, my temporary friend and ally. As one British leader in the 19th century once put it: "Great Britain has no permanent friends. Great Britain has no permanent enemies. Great Britain only has permanent interests."

This belief system was reinforced in the 18th century by mercantilism. Mercantilism is normally associated with the British Navigation Acts of the 17th and 18th centuries, but recent scholarship has argued that it was much more than that, that it was an entire worldview—an ideology, if you will—between the feudalism that had preceded it and the capitalist worldview that followed it. Adam Smith, who wrote the capitalist bible, *The Wealth of Nations*—interestingly, in 1776, the same year as the Declaration of Independence—had labeled this belief system "mercantilism" and had attacked it.

What were the basic principles of mercantilism? [The] first [was] that the best way to obtain, maintain, and organize your national wealth is to create a self-sufficient empire and a favorable balance of trade vis-à-vis other empires. Secondly and critically, the wealth of the world to a mercantilist was finite—not infinite, as it is in capitalism, where wealth can create wealth—but in mercantilism, the wealth of the world is finite. So to gain wealth, you must take it away from somebody else, usually by war, or else they will take it away from you.

These beliefs firmly guided American leaders during the War for Independence, and they established a tradition of realism in foreign policy to balance the idealism that was being simultaneously expressed by Tom Paine and others. The revolutionary leader John Adams argued in 1775 that the French monarchy would help the colonists, despite that monarchy's fear of revolution. Why? Because the primary interest of France was in weakening England, especially in the aftermath of London's stupendous victory in the Seven Years' War.

England and France, in retrospect, were at war for a period of 125 years, running from 1689 to 1815. There were armistice periods in between, but there was war after war after war here. The American War for Independence was part of this struggle, [as] were the wars of the French Revolution, the wars of Napoleon, and as we will see, the American War of 1812. The struggle was for global empire, and Adams argued that France would help the colonists as a means of weakening Britain, but Adams also argued against any formal military alliance with France and against the total destruction of English power. The United States interest, Adams maintained, was to keep these two 18th-century giants, these great powers, balanced against each other and to be aligned with neither of them. Otherwise, he feared, Americans would become, in his famous words, "puppets danced on the wires of the cabinets of Europe." Given these facts, Adams concluded, American negotiators in Paris should confine themselves to a treaty of commerce with France, one containing no political commitments. These terms were written up in a document that Adams authored, which has become known to us as the Model Treaty. It was written to guide American negotiators in Paris. By the terms of the Model Treaty, the United States would offer France its trade on a free or a reciprocal basis in return for French military supplies and naval aid on the high seas.

Future Franco-American trade after this war was to be based on advanced concepts of the rights of neutrals in war, what was known as "freedom of the seas." Free ships make free goods. A neutral would be allowed to trade with both sides as long as the goods carried were not on the contraband list, contraband being the actual implements of war. Adams also defined "contraband" in very narrow terms, essentially guns and ammunition. In addition, the United States was to press for no tariffs, no import taxes on the goods of another country, or if that was not acceptable in this mercantilist world, then a most-favored-nation clause to reduce these tariffs. In a most-favored-nation clause signed by two countries, if any country granted lower tariff rates to a third party, those lower rates would automatically apply to the country that had signed the most-favored-nation agreement.

France was also to give up all land claims in North America—clearly, Adams was thinking the United States would take Canada—but France would be able to reconquer the West Indies islands that it had lost in 1763. If this treaty led to an Anglo-French war—and, of course, it would—the United States promised not to aid England or to sign a separate peace with England.

Adams was absolutely correct about the French being willing to help the Americans in order to weaken England, but the French would demand a military alliance to protect their New World possessions against a British attack or a future American attack. French Foreign Minister [Charles Gravier, comte de] Vergennes, in 1775 (before France agreed to a treaty with the United States), warned in this regard when talking to the British ambassador—that if Americans achieved their independence, they would,

> immediately set about forming a great marine, and as they have every possible advantage for ship-building [it] would not be long before they had such fleets, as would be an overmatch for the whole naval power of Europe. …With this superiority and every advantage of situation they might, when they pleased, conquer both your islands and ours. … They would not stop here [Vergennes warned] but would in process of time advance to the Southern Continent of America and either subdue the inhabitants or carry them along with them, and in the end they would not leave a foot of that Hemisphere in the possession of any European power.

Quite a prophecy, quite a fear.

France would also demand evidence of American military prowess before it signed any treaty with the Americans. Simultaneously, the American colonists would find that they needed far more French aid than originally anticipated to defeat Britain. Let me remind you here that, in 1776, General George Washington had been beaten and humiliated again and again and again in a series of battles, first in the New York area and then in New Jersey. He was on the verge of total defeat by the end of 1776 when he launched his counterattacks at Trenton and Princeton. In 1777, the situation was not that much better.

The result would be the 1778 Treaty of Commerce with France and the 1778 Treaty of Alliance with France. Two treaties are signed, both negotiated by Benjamin Franklin and his colleagues with Vergennes. They are negotiated in the immediate aftermath of the great American military victory at Saratoga, which shows the French that the Americans can, indeed, preserve their independence. The Treaty of Commerce followed the terms of Adams's Model Treaty, but the Treaty of Alliance was another matter. It bound France to fight until American independence was achieved, but it bound the United States to defend the French West Indies indefinitely.

French military assistance would prove critical to the war effort. That had been true secretly even before the treaties. The French had been supplying arms and ammunition to the colonists secretly in 1776 and 1777. At Saratoga, 90 percent of colonial arms and ammunition came from the French. Furthermore, a French army would be sent to North America. The French navy would be involved in American territorial waters. Indeed, Cornwallis's army would be trapped at Yorktown, not merely by George Washington's Continental army but also by a French army and by the French navy. There are more French soldiers and sailors at Yorktown than there are American soldiers and sailors. Furthermore, the addition of France to the war effort diverted the British from North America to the Caribbean in their own war effort.

French diplomacy was also critical; it prevented Britain from obtaining any allies, and it brought Spain and other European nations into the conflict, either as allies of France (though not as formal allies of the United States) or as friendly neutrals. As a result of all of this, Britain found itself in a world war and diplomatically isolated by 1781, and after its defeat at Yorktown, it decided to make peace with the Americans as a means of dividing its enemies and minimizing its losses.

Fearing French manipulation, as Adams had warned, and tempted by generous British terms, the American negotiators—Benjamin Franklin, John Jay, and John Adams—once again practiced realpolitik. They violated the spirit if not the letter of the French alliance by agreeing to separate talks with the British. In those talks, they obtained highly favorable terms. Those terms included not only independence but boundaries that stretched all the way to the Mississippi River. For a while, it looked like they might get part or all of Canada. The British seemed willing, at one point, to negotiate that, but then British victories in the Caribbean led to a tougher British stance, and Canada was not to be included in the new United States.

These Anglo-American talks and these terms, when combined with French and Spanish military defeats that took place after Yorktown, convinced the French and the Spanish to sign a general peace in 1783. The Anglo-American separate peace became part of this general peace. The United States was recognized as an independent nation. Its boundaries were to stretch all the way to the Mississippi River. But, as we are going to see in the next lecture, the Spanish would not agree to the southern boundary between American territory and the territory of Spanish Florida that the British and the Americans had agreed to. They also would not agree to the terms that the British and the Americans had agreed to regarding the Mississippi boundary, as we will see. Furthermore, the British would not fulfill all of the terms of the 1783 peace treaty. That's another story.

The Americans had defeated the greatest empire in the world. They were euphoric, but in their euphoria, they tended to ignore the hardheaded, realistic diplomacy that their negotiators had practiced with the great powers of Europe. Instead, Americans tended to see their success in idealistic terms, as divinely inspired and as destined to result in the remaking of the entire world.

I think this was most clearly expressed by Ezra Stiles, a minister and the president of Yale University, who in a 1783 sermon, argued that the United States was to become the beacon of liberty for the entire world and that its success in the Revolutionary War and ensuing independence were key signs that this nation was—as the Puritans had claimed back in the 1630s—God's new Israel, a covenanted community and a key to the Second Coming. "We live in an age of wonders," said Stiles. "We have lived an age in a few years. We have seen more wonders accomplished in eight years than are usually unfolded in a century." Such beliefs would have a major impact on Americans' future behavior.

Lecture Two
Confederation and the Constitution

Scope:

Throughout the immediate postwar years, the United States existed not as a unified entity but as 13 sovereign and weak states held together in a loose confederation and facing numerous threats to their existence. This lecture analyzes those threats and how they led to the writing and ratification of the Constitution to replace the Articles of Confederation, thereby establishing a new and much stronger form of government capable of conducting a vigorous foreign policy. We will also explore key foreign policy provisions of the Constitution.

Outline

I. Throughout the 1780s, the United States existed not as a single national entity but as 13 largely autonomous states held together in a loose confederation under a frame of government known as the Articles of Confederation. Though 19th-century historians considered the Confederation a failure, 20th-century scholars have rediscovered its numerous successes.

   A. The underappreciated successes of the Confederation government included the 1783 peace treaty that successfully ended the War for Independence; the opening of trade with new areas, such as China; treaties with numerous European nations and Native American tribes; and the Northwest Ordinances.

      1. The Northwest Ordinances became a model for the future territorial expansion of the United States without fear of revolt by colonists, similar to the American revolt against British rule.

      2. The ordinances provided for the creation of states once a certain population had been achieved and their incorporation into the Confederation on a basis of full political equality.

   B. But the Confederation also faced numerous and serious foreign policy problems.

      1. With no authority to tax, the Confederation had no power to raise or maintain a national army.

2. Such an army was needed to enforce treaties that had been signed with the Native American tribes on the frontier and to defend the frontier against the British in the Northwest and the Spanish in the Southwest.
3. In the Northwest, the British refused to evacuate eight forts despite their pledge to do so in the 1783 peace treaty. From those posts, the British supported Native American tribes resisting American settlers.
4. In the Southwest, Spain similarly supported Native American resistance to settlement. Spain also refused to recognize the boundary between the United States and Florida, established in the 1783 peace treaty, and denied the United States both navigation rights on the Mississippi River and the crucial "right of deposit" at the port of New Orleans.
5. Overseas trade also suffered as a result of attacks by the Barbary States of North Africa and London's refusal to grant Americans trading privileges within the mercantilist British Empire, of which they were no longer a part.

C. These foreign policy problems were interwoven with domestic problems of the Confederation.
1. Most states saw conflict between easterners and westerners, with westerners complaining that their interests were not being protected and that they were open to secessionist threats, which were, in turn, encouraged by the Spanish in the Southwest.
2. The Confederation was also weakened by a split between northern states, primarily interested in protection and expansion of overseas commerce, and southern states, primarily interested in protection and expansion of western land.

D. All these issues came together in the statehood bids of Kentucky and Vermont, the Jay-Gardoqui affair of 1785–1786, and the more famous Shays's Rebellion of 1786.

E. The result was a growing apprehension that the Confederation would soon break up, leaving the 13 states weak and divided, much as Europe was, or else that the states would be strangled and devoured by Britain and Spain.

II. Such politicians as James Madison (1751–1836), who had always favored a stronger central government, argued that these problems resulted from the weaknesses of the Confederation and that the entire American experiment in representative government was consequently threatened.

  A. Those in favor of strong central control organized a meeting of state representatives in Philadelphia in 1787 to strengthen the Confederation government.

  B. Instead of amending the Articles of Confederation to strengthen that government, the representatives in Philadelphia decided to write a constitution that would create an entirely new form of government, the one under which we live today.

  C. All agreed on the need to expand the power of the national government in four areas directly related to foreign affairs: taxation, establishment of a military, regulation of foreign commerce, and treaty enforcement.

  D. Problems emerged as a result of the existing split between the northern and southern states, as well as the fear that too much centralized power would destroy liberty and lead to a new tyranny.

  E. The North-South differences were resolved in a series of compromises on commercial legislation, export and import taxes, votes on treaties, and a 20-year protection for the slave trade.

  F. The fear of too much centralized power was dealt with through the checks and balances within the new federal system established by the Constitution.

    1. That document established a single executive with authority in foreign and military affairs, but that authority had to be shared with the legislative branch via the "separation of powers."

    2. Furthermore, powers not granted to the new national government were to be reserved for the states via the "division of powers," thereby creating a federated system of representative government instead of the confederation that had previously existed.

III. In the process of structuring the new government, the writers of the Constitution stood established political theory on its head and created the foundation for an expanding empire based on liberty.

    A. Established political theory held that representative government worked best for small states, while large ones required more centralized power in the form of a monarchy.

    B. James Madison, the primary author of the Constitution, argued that representative government would work better in a large and expanding nation than in a small one and that liberty could, thereby, be reconciled with great-power status.

    C. Madison's argument became a core belief in America's rise to superpower status, while his document, the Constitution, became the means to that rise through its creation of a new national government with a strong executive able to exercise power in the international arena.

Suggested Readings:

Marks, *Independence on Trial*.

Morris, *The Forging of the Union*.

Questions to Consider:

1. Did the problems experienced under the Articles of Confederation truly result in a "critical" period in U.S. history, as early historians maintained, or have these problems been overstated?

2. What led writers of the Constitution to believe that their document could resolve the problems of the Confederation period without destroying liberty at home?

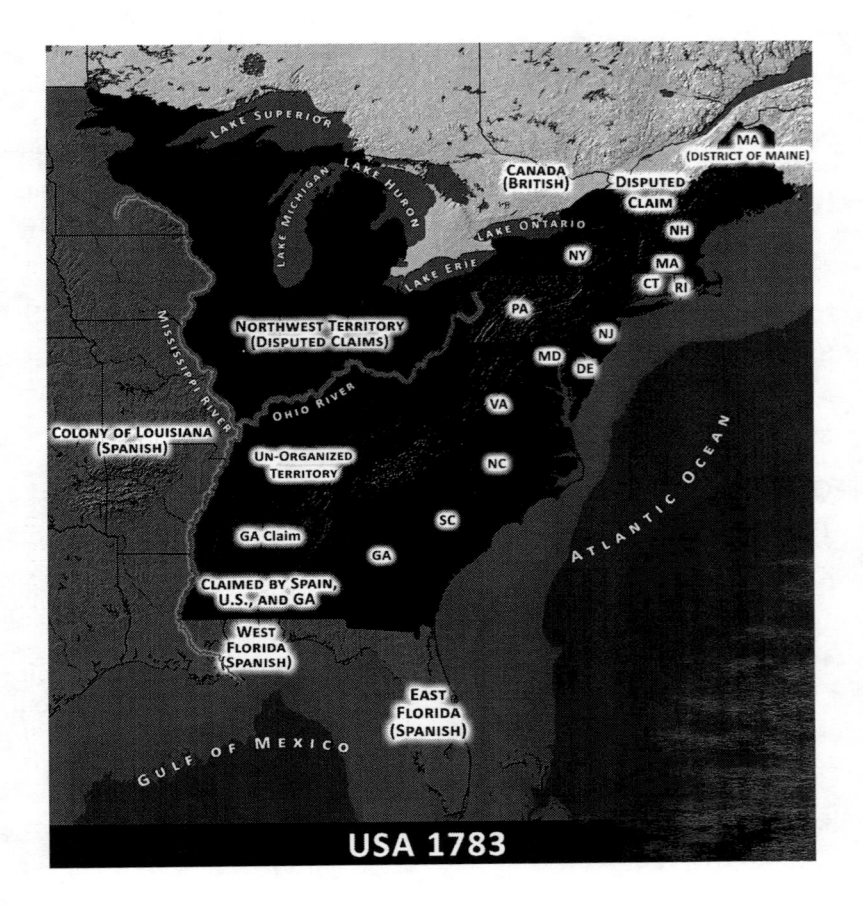

Lecture Two—Transcript
Confederation and the Constitution

Throughout the 1780s, the United States existed not as a single nation but as 13 largely independent states held together in a loose confederation under a frame of government known as the Articles of Confederation. In this system, each of the 13 states maintained its sovereignty, with only a Confederation Congress holding them together. In that Congress, each state had one vote, with any important action requiring at least 9 out of the 13 to vote yes and no executive power to enforce any decision of that group. In retrospect, I think we can say that this frame of government had greater similarity to the contemporary United Nations than to the national government we live under today.

In the late 19th century, historians argued that this time period had constituted a "critical era." When the Confederation government proved simply incapable of running the country, indeed, you didn't have a country. In this interpretation, the Founding Fathers and their Constitution emerge as the salvation, the God-like Founding Fathers who come up with this perfect document.

In the 20th century, that interpretation was attacked by other scholars, who pointed out numerous things. For the purposes of our course, the critical fact they pointed out was that the era was not as terrible and "critical" as these earlier historians claimed, that indeed, there were numerous successes of the United States under the Confederation government, successes that historians have rediscovered and claim have been deeply underappreciated.

Well, what were these in terms of foreign policy? For a start, the 1783 Treaty of Peace that ended successfully the War for Independence took place under the Articles of Confederation. You also had major trade expansion during the 1780s and the opening of trade with previously closed nations in Europe, as well as your first ships traveling to China and the opening of trade with Asia. You had treaties with numerous European nations, not only France but the Netherlands, Sweden, and Prussia. In the Mediterranean, there was a treaty with Morocco, and there were numerous treaties with Indian tribes.

Perhaps of greatest importance for the future rise of American power, you had the passage of the Northwest Ordinances during the 1780s, which established rules by which the huge territory north of the Ohio River—territory that had been claimed by individual states—that those states gave up their claims to the Confederation government [and established] rules by which this large territory was to be divided, settled, and governed. The importance of these Northwest Ordinances cannot be overstated. In retrospect, they provided the model for future additional territorial expansion without fear of colonial revolts in the western territories similar to the revolt that produced the independent United States in 1776.

Americans were aware that colonial subjects resented being colonial subjects and would rebel against this. How do you expand and prevent yourself from facing such revolts? You do so by providing for the admission of these western territories as new states into the Union on a basis of full political equality with the existing 13 states. Future U.S. territorial expansion and the maintenance of a country as large as the United States would, in all likelihood, not have been possible without these ordinances and the pattern they established for admission not only of the states north of the Ohio River but for the new states that were then added from territories acquired west of the Mississippi River.

Despite these successes, the Confederation did face numerous and serious foreign policy problems. What were they? The Confederation government had no power to tax. With no power to tax, it had no power to raise or maintain a national army, nor did it have an executive to control any such army if such an army had existed. But that brings up an obvious question: Why would such an army be needed, given the fact that the War for Independence was over? Would it be needed? The answer is yes.

You needed a national army to enforce treaties with the Indian tribes on the frontier. The Confederation government had no power to enforce such treaties. It had no power to stop white violations of these treaties or state violations of these treaties or to stop the retaliatory Indian attacks that took place when Indians concluded that their rights were being violated. You also needed an army to defend the frontier against the British in Canada and against the Spanish in Florida, in Louisiana, and as we shall see, elsewhere.

In the Northwest, the British were violating the 1783 peace treaty by refusing to evacuate eight forts, known as the Northwest Posts, on American territory. From these forts, they were also supporting Indian tribes who were resisting American settlers. Spain similarly supported Indian tribes resisting American settlers in the South and the Southwest. Spain also refused to recognize that the boundary between the United States and Spanish Florida was at the 31st degree north latitude, as in the peace treaty that the Americans and the British had signed. The Spanish claimed it was the 33rd parallel north latitude. The confusion came from the fact that Spain had controlled Florida until the Seven Years' War, at which time Britain obtained control of Florida and held it until the American War for Independence and, in the 1783 treaty, gave Florida back to Spain— but which Florida and at what boundary?

Spain also denied the United States the right to navigate the Mississippi River and the crucial "right of deposit" at New Orleans. There were virtually no roads across the Allegheny Mountains. Any settlers living west of the Alleghenies would get their goods to market—their produce to market—by going down the Ohio/ Mississippi River system, usually by raft. The goods then needed to be deposited at New Orleans and placed on oceangoing vessels. Without the right of deposit at New Orleans, settlers west of the Alleghenies could not economically survive.

Furthermore, with independence, the United States was now suddenly shut out of trade with the mercantilist British Empire, save on unfavorable British terms that resulted in a serious balance-of-payments deficit for the 13 states. Furthermore, the United States no longer had the protection of the British navy against the Barbary States in the Mediterranean, states that now captured U.S. ships and seamen and demanded ransom and/or tribute.

These foreign policy problems tied into domestic problems of the Confederation government in this era. In most states, you had a conflict of easterners versus westerners, with westerners complaining that their interests were being ignored and their security was not being protected. These were followed by secessionist threats in the West, which the Spanish encouraged in the Southwest. You had during this time the so-called Spanish Conspiracy in Kentucky and Tennessee, with Revolutionary War General James Wilkinson being secretly in the pay of the Spanish government. He was receiving a

Spanish pension, as well as trade privileges, and was being directed to promote secessionist tendencies in this area. He is one of the great traitors in American history. His treason was not discovered, however, until after his death, and we will be coming back to him, as we will see.

You also had a North/South split between the states over foreign policy. Northeastern commercial and shipping interests wanted protection and expansion of overseas commerce. They wanted to break into the European mercantilist systems. Southerners were more interested in the protection and expansion of western lands—lands that they needed for speculation (because their tobacco cash crop wore out the soil)—to preserve the North/South balance in the Confederation Congress and to block the intrigues of the Spanish. The northeastern states opposed this, fearing dilution of their power.

All of these issues came together in a series of disturbing events in the 1780s. Kentucky, which had been part of Virginia, asked Virginia for separate status as a separate state. Virginia agreed. The belief system at the time, as we will explore a little later in this lecture, is that republic[an] representative governments only could survive in small areas. Virginia agreed to the separation of Kentucky if Kentucky would be admitted to the Confederation as the 14th state, but the northeastern states blocked this. They feared dilution of their power, and that only encouraged the secessionist plots in Kentucky further.

Vermont also desired admission to the Union as a state, but New York and New Hampshire blocked this. Indeed, New York and New Hampshire claimed [that] Vermont did not exist, that the lands making up Vermont belonged to New York and New Hampshire. Vermont responded by claiming [that] portions of New York and New Hampshire belonged to itself and—with its own version of secessionist threat—negotiated with the British in Canada in return for trade privileges.

Then, in 1785, you had the Jay-Gardoqui affair. Don Diego de Gardoqui, Spanish emissary, came to the United States and offered John Jay—at this point, the foreign minister of the Confederation Congress—trading privileges in the Spanish Empire, the 31st degree north latitude as the boundary between the United States and Spanish Florida, and Spain's support against the British and the Barbary States if, in return, the United States gave up the right to navigate the Mississippi River. Jay was from the Northeast, New York. He agreed to this, albeit for a limited period of time. For 25 to 30 years, the United States, he said, would forbear use of the Mississippi, rather than giving it up. But he asked Congress to alter his diplomatic instructions so as to allow this. The southern states exploded. There was talk of disunion. The measure was able to pass by a seven-to-five vote, but that, in effect, ended the negotiations because Jay realized that he could never muster the nine votes needed to pass this, and the uproar that was being caused by this threatened disunion.

On top of all of this came Shays's Rebellion in western Massachusetts; that was a purely domestic issue. Shays's Rebellion was the revolt of disgruntled farmers in western Massachusetts to stop foreclosures on their farms that were being caused by the economic depression at that time. There was no national army to send in to put down the rebellion. There was the Massachusetts state militia, but it was uncertain. These were the fellow citizens, the neighbors. Would they stop Shays's Rebellion, or would they join it? They stopped it, but it raised the question, and without a national army, the belief arose that the Confederation was showing that it could not keep internal—nor, as we have seen in foreign policy, could it keep external—order. Indeed, many linked the internal problems to the external problems. The economic depression that had led to the foreclosures and the rebellion in western Massachusetts had been caused by a depression blamed on the inability of the Confederation government to secure trading privileges with the European empires.

James Madison wrote at this time: "Most of our political evils may be traced ... to our commercial ones, [and] most of our moral may to our political." The result was a growing apprehension that the Confederation was about to break up and leave 13 states weak and divided, much as Europe was divided, or that these 13 states would be totally devoured by Britain and by Spain. Either way, the entire American experiment in liberty and in representative government was perceived as being in mortal danger.

The obvious solution was a stronger central government, but how do you create a stronger central government given the internal splits I have just described and the fact that you had just fought a war against a strong central government in Great Britain and see a strong central government as the greatest threat to liberty on the basis of your own experiences? Now, those in favor of such a stronger central government were able to obtain agreement that there should be a meeting of representatives in Philadelphia in 1787 to amend and strengthen the Articles of Confederation. But once those representatives met, they decided not to amend and strengthen the articles but to write an entirely new frame of government, to throw the articles out the window—windows, by the way, that they sealed so as to keep their negotiations secret. And they wrote the Constitution under which we live to this very day.

In Philadelphia, the delegates all agreed on the need to expand national power in four key areas related to foreign affairs: taxation, raising an army and a navy, regulation of commerce, and enforcement of treaties. But within, as well as beyond, that, problems emerged as a result of the existing North/South split that I previously described and the fear that any new centralized power could destroy liberty at home.

The North/South splits were resolved by a series of compromises. No taxes were ever to be allowed on exports. Commercial legislation would be decided by majority vote in the new national legislature, but treaties would require a two-thirds positive vote in the Senate to prevent another Jay-Gardoqui affair. In addition, the South would find the slave trade protected for 20 years. The slave trade could not be touched for 20 years.

The fear of tyrannical central power was more complex, and this would be dealt with by the complex series of checks and balances within the new federal system of government that the Constitution established. To call the national government "the federal government" is, in a sense, a misnomer. As we will see, "federal" has a different meaning. "Federal" is the division of power between the new national government and the state governments.

But the whole idea here of what you were going to do was best summed up by James Madison, the father of the Constitution, in a document that he wrote to help New Yorkers vote for the Constitution. These were the Federalist Papers that he coauthored with John Jay and Alexander Hamilton. In Federalist No. 51, James Madison wrote the following regarding the fear versus the need of central government:

If men were angels, no government would be necessary. If angels were to govern men, neither external nor internal controls on government would be necessary. In framing a government which is to be administered by men over men, the great difficulty lies in this: you must first enable the government to control the governed; and in the next place oblige it to control itself.

How?

The method to control the national government is the system we know as checks and balances. These need to be explained on two levels: the separation of powers and the division of powers. The separation of powers refers to the three branches of the new national government: the executive, the legislative, and the judicial. A single executive, the president of the United States, is established with very strong powers in foreign and military affairs. The president is to be the commander in chief of the army and navy of the United States and of the militia of the several states when called into actual service of the United States. The president also has the power to make treaties and to appoint ambassadors, consuls, and other diplomatic and military officials.

These powers are shared with the legislative branch; Congress, not the president, has a series of powers here. The Senate must approve presidential appointments and all treaties by a two-thirds vote. The Congress has the power to lay and collect taxes, to coin money, to pay debts, and to "provide for the common defense and general welfare." The Congress has the power to regulate commerce with other nations, and with Indian tribes, and among the states. The Congress, not the president, has the power to declare war, to grant letters of marque and reprisal, and to make rules concerning captures on land and water. It is the Congress that must raise and support armies, with no appropriation lasting for more than two years. It is the Congress that must provide and maintain a navy and make rules for the government and the regulation of the land and naval forces for the United States. The Congress provides for calling forth the state militia to execute the laws of the Union; to suppress insurrection and repel invasion; and to provide for the organizing, arming, and disciplining of the militia. The Congress also has the power to pass whatever laws are "necessary and proper" to execute these enumerated powers.

Furthermore, powers not granted to the new national government are reserved for the states via the division of powers, the militia being a classic example. The militias remain state military forces, with the Congress having the power to establish rules for their training and their use when called into actual national service. In short, what is established here is a federated system of representative government to replace the Confederation that had previously existed. But the new national government, which we call the "federal government," is given exclusive authority over foreign policy. The states are prohibited from making treaties [or] alliances; passing import or export taxes; maintaining troops or ships of war in times of peace, save for the militia; or engaging in war unless invaded.

In establishing such a system of government, the writers of the Constitution stood established political theory on its head. Established political theory held that representative government, known as republican government, worked best in small states. Large states required more centralized power, i.e., a monarchy. James Madison, as primary author of the Constitution, disagreed. In Federalist No. 10, he argued that representative government would work better in a large and expanding nation than it would in a small one.

Madison's logic was based on his definition of factionalism as the key problem. A "faction" he defined as "a group of people, be it a minority or a majority, willing to ride roughshod over the rights of others to obtain its own interests." This would be tyranny. Madison distinguished [among] liberty in representative government, republican government, and democratic government. He and others of his era defined democracy as mob rule, majority rule with no protection for minority rights, and in Federalist No. 10, as much of a threat as an aristocratic elite taking power. What he argued in Federalist No. 10 was that the larger the country, the greater the number of interests or factions, the lesser the chance that any one faction could gain control of the entire government.

As he put it:

> The greater number of citizens and extent of territory which may be brought within the compass of republican than of democratic government; [and it is] this circumstance principally ... renders factious combinations less to be dreaded in the former than in the latter. The smaller the

society, [he wrote] the fewer probably will be the distinct parties and interests composing it; the fewer the distinct parties and interests, the more frequently will a majority be found of the same party; and the smaller the number of individuals composing a majority, and the smaller the compass within which they are placed, the more easily will they concert and execute their plans of oppression.

Extend the sphere, and you take in a greater variety of parties and interests; you make it less probable that a majority of the whole will have a common motive to invade the rights of other citizens; or if such a common motive exists, it will be more difficult for all who feel it to discover their own strength, and to act in unison with each other.

In making such an argument, Madison, in effect, argued that liberty could be reconciled with expansion and with great-power status, that indeed, expansion and great-power status were necessary to preserve liberty. Madison's argument in this regard became a core belief in America's rise to superpower status. His document, the Constitution of the United States, would become the primary means to achieve that rise to power via its creation of a new national government with a strong executive able to exercise power in the international arena.

But could liberty and representative government, in reality, coexist with a strong executive and great-power status? Was Madison's argument the valid one? This is a question Americans have grappled with for over 200 years, and they continue to grapple with it today. Indeed, that question would now split the very individuals who had written the Constitution and who had played so important a role in obtaining its ratification within each state.

Most notable in this regard would be the totally unexpected split that now occurred between the three men who had written the Federalist Papers to help convince New York voters to ratify the Constitution—on one side, Alexander Hamilton and John Jay, and on the other side, James Madison and, as we will see, Thomas Jefferson. The result in the next decade would be major disputes over interpretation of the Constitution, as well as appropriate domestic policies and foreign policies for the new nation to follow.

These disputes would further endanger the young nation and would lead to something none of the Founding Fathers had anticipated or written into the Constitution—permanent political national parties, what we live with today. There is no clause in the Constitution to account for this. When Madison spoke of factions in Federalist No. 10, he was thinking of temporary factions, and he was thinking of them acting individually, rather than coalescing as they would into permanent national political parties. Those would form in the 1790s, and it would be a time period that would constitute one of the most critical times in the history of the young nation. The splits would take place in terms of domestic policy, in terms of constitutional theory, and in terms of foreign policy. These were all linked together, and it is to these splits and the linkage between the different factors that we must now turn.

Lecture Three
The Great Debate—Jefferson versus Hamilton

Scope:

George Washington's presidency witnessed a series of foreign policy crises, stemming from the French Revolution and the resulting war in Europe, that split his key advisers and eventually led to the formation of two national political parties: the Federalists and the Democratic-Republicans. This lecture explores those crises and the very different policies to deal with them proposed by Washington's two key cabinet officers: Treasury Secretary Alexander Hamilton and Secretary of State Thomas Jefferson. So polarized were those policies as to constitute one of the most fundamental disagreements in the history of the nation—and one of the most dangerous. Indeed, they resulted in fierce partisan battles that threatened to rip the country apart, and they prompted Washington's famous Farewell Address, one of the most misunderstood documents and warnings in American history.

Outline

I.   The establishment of the new national government under George Washington (1732–1799) in the 1790s would coincide with the French Revolution and the outbreak of a new war in Europe.

   A. These events led to a massive and fundamental debate within Washington's cabinet and throughout the country over the proper foreign policy for the United States to pursue.

   B. Within the cabinet, this debate pitted Treasury Secretary Alexander Hamilton (1755–1804) against Secretary of State Thomas Jefferson (1743–1826).

   C. By the end of Washington's presidency, it had resulted in the division of the Founders and the country as a whole into two national political parties.

   D. This dispute also constituted one of the most fundamental and dangerous disagreements in American history.

II. Understanding this conflict requires an analysis of the competing visions Hamilton and Jefferson held of what the United States could and should be.

A. Hamilton believed that the United States could, in time, become the dominant power in the Western Hemisphere, but at the moment, the country was weak. Consequently, the immediate tasks were to stay out of the European war and build up American power and influence.

   1. Achieving these goals would involve building up the power of the central government by paying off U.S. debts while fostering commerce and industry.

   2. To accomplish this, Hamilton proposed funding the national debt at par value, assuming the state debts, and establishing internal and external taxes, as well as a national bank.

   3. Close relations with Great Britain were crucial to this plan because the United States critically needed British capital, manufacturers, and trade for the plan to work.

   4. Furthermore, Hamilton argued, Britain was the only country that could seriously hurt the United States. Consequently, the United States should unofficially align with the British.

   5. Hamilton was quite conservative ideologically and deeply distrusted the radical doctrines of the French Revolution. But he developed and promoted his policies before that revolution turned radical in 1793 and led to war between republican France and the monarchs of Europe.

B. Jefferson and his close collaborator, James Madison, thoroughly disagreed and proposed a sharply different vision of the United States and its foreign policies.

   1. Jefferson and Madison were southern agrarians who were deeply distrustful of concentrated power in any form and, thus, were opposed to a nation based on commerce and industry.

   2. They also objected to the fact that funding and assumption would favor northern banking interests over southern agrarian interests.

3. Furthermore, they believed that Britain desired the destruction or permanent dependence of the United States and had the power to achieve it.
4. Although the United States was weak at this time, Jefferson and Madison believed that it possessed the economic power to force British concessions and to do so without resort to war.
5. The United States could also wring concessions from, and avoid dependence on, Great Britain by maintaining close commercial and political relations with France, thereby using France as a counterweight to British power.
6. As with Hamilton, Jefferson developed this position before the 1793 radicalization of the French Revolution and ensuing war between republican France and the monarchs of Europe. But whereas Hamilton distrusted and feared radical French ideology, Jefferson saw the French Revolution as related to the American Revolution and as another step in the global republican revolution that the United States had begun and had a mission to support and spread.

C. The question of whether this disagreement pitted Hamiltonian Realism against Jeffersonian Idealism or represented distinctions far more complex and nuanced has long divided historians and continues to do so.

III. The Hamilton-Jefferson division emerged in a series of major policy disagreements between 1789 and 1795.

A. First came the import tax and Nootka Sound controversies, but these were only preliminaries to the major debate that then occurred over the appropriate American response to the new French Republic and the ensuing war in Europe.
1. Hamilton and Jefferson agreed that the United States should remain neutral in this conflict but disagreed as to how that neutrality should be specifically implemented.
2. Hamilton argued that the 1778 Treaty of Alliance with France should be considered suspended because it had been signed with a government that had now been overthrown and that neutrality should be proclaimed immediately. He also argued that the envoy of the new

French Republic, Citizen Edmond-Charles Genêt, should not be received.

3. Jefferson argued for receiving Genêt and against any immediate suspension of the alliance or declaration of neutrality, moves that Britain desired and should be forced to pay for via evacuation of the Northwest Posts.

4. Washington compromised on April 22 by issuing a neutrality proclamation, as Hamilton had recommended, but refusing to declare the treaty suspended and agreeing to receive Genêt, as Jefferson had recommended. He and Jefferson thereby established two key precedents in American foreign policy: *de facto* recognition of any government that exercised power and the sanctity of treaties.

B. Genêt sought to turn the United States into a base of operations for French privateering, and when Washington and Jefferson objected, he appealed over their heads to the American people. The move backfired and resulted in a blast of anti-French sentiment.

C. At the same time, relations with England seriously deteriorated owing to the continued British occupation of the Northwest Posts, support for the Native American tribes in their war against the United States, and British assaults on U.S. neutral rights and ships on the high seas—moves that many Americans perceived as a coordinated effort to destroy the United States on land and sea.

D. Fearing war, Washington and Hamilton decided to send Supreme Court Chief Justice John Jay (1745–1829) to England in an effort to resolve these problems.

1. The British agreed to abandon the Northwest posts as a result of the U.S. military victory against the Northwest Indian Confederation at the 1794 Battle of Fallen Timbers, followed by the Treaty of Greenville in 1795, in which the tribes surrendered extensive land in Ohio.

2. In return, however, Jay had to agree to the British definition of neutral rights.

E. Jay's Treaty was one of the first and most important treaties negotiated by the new nation.

    1. On the positive side, it ensured a decade of peace with Great Britain and helped open the Old Northwest to American settlers.

    2. On the negative side, the treaty surrendered the American position on neutral rights in terms that were both insulting and humiliating.

    3. Those terms were also sectional and partisan, undercutting Jefferson's foreign policy and leading to both a public uproar and a constitutional crisis.

    4. The treaty thus became the single most important event in the formation of two national political parties: the Federalists, led by Washington, Adams, and Hamilton and identified as pro-British, and the Democratic-Republicans, led by Jefferson and Madison and identified as pro-French.

F. The treaty would also have significant additional consequences for the United States over the rest of the decade, including spawning a major treaty with Spain, Washington's Farewell Address, an undeclared war with France, and a near civil war.

Suggested Readings:

Combs, *The Jay Treaty*.

DeConde, *Entangling Alliance*.

Ellis, *Founding Brothers*.

Kohn, *Eagle and Sword*.

Varg, *Foreign Policies of the Founding Fathers*.

Questions to Consider:

1. To what extent were the Jefferson-Hamilton differences over appropriate foreign policies the result of: (a) different assessments of the international situation and American power, (b) differences over appropriate domestic policies, (c) sectional interests, (d) conflicting interpretations of the Constitution, and (e) conflicting political philosophies and ideologies?

2. Why did the Jay Treaty have such far-reaching consequences?

Lecture Three—Transcript
The Great Debate—Jefferson versus Hamilton

The establishment of the new national government under the Constitution, with George Washington unanimously elected first president, would coincide with the French Revolution and the outbreak of a new war in Europe by 1793. That, in turn, would lead to a massive and fundamental debate within George Washington's cabinet and within the country as a whole over the proper foreign policy for the United States to pursue.

Within the cabinet, it pitted Treasury Secretary Alexander Hamilton against Secretary of State Thomas Jefferson. By the end of Washington's presidency, the debate would result in something the writers of the Constitution had neither envisaged nor desired—(as previously noted) their division and the division of the country as a whole into two permanent national political parties.

The debate also constituted one of the most fundamental disagreements in all of American history—and as we will see, one of the most dangerous—for the two sides held very different and conflicting visions of what the United States could and should do in foreign affairs, visions inextricably tied to their conflicting domestic policies, their sectional interests, and their general philosophies. Differences so fundamental threatened to rip the nation apart. To understand these differences, we must look at the domestic, sectional, and philosophical differences in order to understand the differences over foreign policy.

Alexander Hamilton first: Hamilton is often seen as the classic realist in foreign policy. He believed that the United States could, in time, become the dominant power in the Western Hemisphere, [but] that at this moment, it was very weak and vulnerable. Consequently, he argued, the immediate tasks were to stay out of European war and to build up American power and influence. Hamilton argued that this would require the building up of power and influence of the new national government by having that government pay off U.S. debts from the Revolutionary War while fostering commerce and industry at home. He called for funding the national debt at par value—in other words, paying off the national debt with new securities at the value that purchasers had paid for these securities during the Revolutionary War, as opposed to the depreciated value that those securities held by the 1790s. In other words, if you had, as a patriotic duty, bought a Revolutionary War bond for $100, that bond was not worth $100 on the open market in the 1790s. Hamilton said, "I will pay off the $100." He also wanted the new national government to assume state debts, and he wanted Congress to pass new internal and external taxes to pay for all of this and to establish a national bank— partially owned by the national government and partially owned by private bankers—to administer the entire system.

What does any of this have to do with foreign policy? Close relations with Great Britain were crucial to Hamilton's entire plan. British capital, British manufacturers, and British trade were vital for this plan to work. Taxes on imports provided the bulk of government revenues at this time, and it was those revenues that were going to pay off the national and state debts. Britain supplied 90 percent of U.S. imports and, thus, paid the bulk of the import taxes that would pay off this debt. Britain also took half of all U.S. exports. In fact, three-quarters of all U.S. trade was with Great Britain. The prosperity of the country, as well as the ability of the new government to pay off its debt, depended upon this trade. Hamilton also argued that Britain was the only country that could seriously hurt the United States, so the United States should unofficially align with Britain and do nothing that might lead to conflict with that country. Hamilton was also quite conservative ideologically. He deeply distrusted and feared the radical doctrines of the French Revolution, but Hamilton developed and promoted his policies before the French Revolution turned radical in 1793 and led to war between republican France and the monarchs of Europe.

What about Jefferson and his close collaborator, James Madison, who at this point is in the House of Representatives? Jefferson and Madison thoroughly disagreed with Hamilton and proposed a sharply different vision of the United States and its foreign policies. Partially, this was due to the fact that they came from the South, whereas Hamilton came from the North. As southern agrarians, they did not want a nation based on Hamilton's vision of commerce and industry. Furthermore, funding and assumption would favor northern banking interests, which had purchased the depreciated securities, over southern agrarian interests. Ideologically, Jefferson and Madison also distrusted concentrated power in any form whatsoever and, thus, did not want the powerful national government that Hamilton was trying to create, nor did they want close relations with the very powerful British, whom they distrusted even more because of [their] power.

Jefferson and Madison agreed with Hamilton that the British were the only power that could hurt the United States, but they believed that that was exactly what London wanted to do—not simply to hurt the United States but to destroy it, to undo the results of the revolution or to make the young nation permanently dependent upon Great Britain. They also believed that Britain had the power to obtain the destruction or dependence of the United States via the continued American reliance on British trade, as well as the continued British occupation of the Northwest Posts. From their point of view, Hamilton's policy constituted (to use a contemporary term) appeasement of a tyrannical power that would destroy the independence of the United States. What the United States needed to do was avoid economic reliance on Britain and force Britain out of the Northwest Posts.

Jefferson and Madison clearly did agree with Hamilton that the United States was weak at this time, but unlike Hamilton, they believed that the United States did possess the economic power to force concessions from Great Britain and to do so without resort to war. How? Britain, they argued, needed our trade more than we needed theirs. The British West Indies, totally devoted to producing cash crops, were totally dependent on American foodstuffs. So, to an extent, were the British Isles. Therefore, use the threat of economic retaliation against Britain—what is often referred to as "peaceable coercion"—to wring concessions from London. Hamilton believed that this was utter nonsense and would lead to war.

Jefferson also believed that the United States could wring concessions from Great Britain and avoid dependence on that power by maintaining close commercial and political relations with France, using France as a counterweight to British power. An interesting analogy to understand this might be the position of third world countries during the Cold War that claimed neutrality because they did not want to become dependent on either of the two giants: the United States or the Soviet Union. The United States was in that position, the position of a weak third world country with two giants, in the late 18th century.

As with Hamilton, Jefferson and Madison developed this position before the 1793 radicalization of the French Revolution and the ensuing war between republican France and the monarchs of Europe. But whereas Hamilton distrusted and feared radical French ideology, Jefferson did not. To the contrary, he saw the French Revolution as related to the American Revolution and as another step in the global republican revolution that the United States had begun and that it had a mission to support and spread throughout the world.

Did this disagreement really pit Hamiltonian "Realism" against Jeffersonian "Idealism," or were the distinctions far more complex and nuanced? Historians have long disagreed on this, and they continue to do so. My own point of view is that the idealist/realist dichotomy is much too simplistic. Hamilton is admittedly more a disciple of Thomas Hobbes, and Jefferson more a disciple of John Locke in terms of worldviews, but both were willing to play balance-of-power politics, albeit in different ways. Furthermore, as we will see in detail in later lectures, Jefferson, in effect, will fuse self-interest with his idealism, thereby coming up with an ideology. Some scholars have labeled Jefferson as the first ideologue to hold power in the United States. Again, we'll be going into this in greater depth as the course progresses, but however one views the disagreement between Hamilton and Jefferson, it is one of the most fundamental in all of American history. Its outcome would play a critical role in the survival of the United States during this time and its eventual emergence as a superpower.

The division first emerged in a series of major policy disagreements running from about 1789 to 1795. You had, for example, the import controversy. Madison, in the House of Representatives, proposed a bill for economic retaliation against Great Britain. Hamilton had his supporters in the Senate defeat this bill. In 1790, in the so-called Nootka Sound controversy, the possibility of war between Britain and Spain emerged. Spain was aligned with France. The war never happened, but Washington feared that it would, and he asked the cabinet what to do if the British wanted to cross U.S. territory in order to attack the Spanish in Louisiana. Hamilton said: "Agree; you cannot stop the British, and a British attack upon the Spanish could open the Mississippi River." Jefferson said that would make Britain even more of a threat than it presently was. Here was Britain in control of Canada and the Northwest Posts; now, you're going to allow Britain to gain control of the Mississippi River, Louisiana, and

New Orleans? Jefferson argued that the American answer should be no until Britain agreed to give up the Northwest Posts. Furthermore, he argued, the United States should threaten economic retaliation against Britain, as well as [the development of] closer relations with France.

As I stated, war never came about, so the issue became moot. These were preliminaries to the major debate that occurred in 1793 over the appropriate response to the new French Republic and the ensuing war in Europe. Hamilton and Jefferson did agree that the United States should remain neutral in that war, but they disagreed as to how that neutrality should be specifically implemented in light of the still-existing 1778 Treaty of Alliance with France. Remember, that treaty from the American War for Independence is still in existence. The United States is officially allied with France and bound to defend the French West Indies.

In the cabinet, Hamilton argued that the treaty should be considered suspended on the grounds that it had been signed with a previous government, a government now overthrown. Neutrality should be proclaimed immediately, and the United States should refuse to receive the new envoy that republican France was sending to the United States, Edmond Genêt.

Jefferson countered that treaties are with nations, not with particular governments. France is still a nation; therefore, he concluded, the United States should receive Genêt. It should not announce any suspension of the alliance, [and] it should not declare neutrality unless and until Britain first evacuated the Northwest Posts—i.e., [if] Britain wants us to announce the suspension of the treaty and declare neutrality, make them pay for what they want. Don't give it to them for nothing.

Washington decided to compromise. On April 22, 1793, he issued a Neutrality Proclamation, as Hamilton had recommended, but he refused to declare the Treaty of Alliance suspended and he agreed to receive Genêt, as Jefferson had recommended. In doing so, Washington and Jefferson had thereby established two key precedents in the history of U.S. foreign policy: *de facto* recognition of any government that actually exercises power and the sanctity of existing treaties. The recognition of any government that exercises power would last until Woodrow Wilson changed it in 1913, something we will deal with later in this course.

Edmond Genêt [was] a diplomatic amateur who called himself "Citizen" Genêt. (Part of the republican revolution in France was that you would become citizens instead of subjects; I guess the equivalent during the era of the Soviet Union was use of the term "comrade.") [Genêt] tried to turn the United States into a base of operations for French privateering. Washington and Jefferson both objected, and when they did so, Genêt threatened to appeal over their heads to the American people. That move backfired tremendously: It resulted in a blast of anti-French sentiment and the request by Jefferson and Washington that Genêt be recalled as *persona non grata*. The French government agreed to that, but by this time, Genêt's group was out of power, and a more radical group had come in. The Reign of Terror was in full force, and Genêt, if he did return, would lose his head. He begged for permission to remain in the United States. Washington granted it to him, and he then sank into—as one historian has put it—"the obscurity he so richly deserved."

At the same time, relations with England deteriorated seriously due to continued British occupation of the Northwest Posts and support for the Indian tribes in their war against the United States. Washington sent two military expeditions into the Northwest; both were defeated by the Indian tribes. The whole frontier was being rolled back. Furthermore, the British were accused of aiding these Indians and were assaulting United States rights and ships on the high seas. They were also impressing seamen from American merchant ships into the British navy, something we will deal with in greater depth when we get to the War of 1812. Many Americans saw all of this as a coordinated effort by England to destroy the United States on land and sea.

Fearing war, Washington and Hamilton decided to send Supreme Court Chief Justice John Jay to London in an effort to resolve all Anglo-American problems. Jay was aided by the fact that the third military expedition sent in against the Northwest Indians (this time under General Anthony Wayne in 1794) succeeded. The famous Battle of Fallen Timbers marked Wayne's defeat of the Indian confederation in the Northwest, and it was followed a year later, in 1795, by the Treaty of Greenville, in which the tribes were forced to surrender extensive land in present-day Ohio.

Consequently, the British agreed to abandon the Northwest Posts and, temporarily, their efforts to incite the Indian tribes in the area. But in return for this, Jay had to agree to the British definition of neutral rights, giving up the traditional American definition that John Adams had put into the Model Treaty.

The Treaty of London—or Jay's Treaty, as it is called—ranks as one of the first and most important treaties the new national government would negotiate. On the positive side, it ensured a decade of peace with Great Britain at a time when the United States was weak, and it helped to open the Old Northwest to American settlers. But for those gains, Jay had to surrender the United States position on neutral rights in terms that were both insulting and humiliating. Instead of the narrow definition of contraband that the French had agreed to in their Treaty of Commerce, Jay had to agree to a broad British definition of contraband that included material used indirectly to make war. He also had to agree to very limited American trade with the British West Indies and to arbitration so that British creditors could be compensated for their losses from before the Revolutionary War. He had to give up the whole concept of "free ships make free goods." French goods on U.S. ships could be seized. Food bound for France could be seized. Washington even considered not submitting the treaty to the Senate. He eventually did, and he tried to keep the terms secret. That effort failed, as we will see.

The terms of the Jay Treaty were also sectional and partisan in that they undercut Jefferson's proposed foreign policy. The Jay Treaty included a reciprocity clause and a most-favored-nation clause. That meant that economic retaliation against Britain was no longer possible. The Senate ratified the treaty—barely. The vote was 20 to 10, but the public uproar that ensued when the terms became known was unprecedented. "Damn John Jay," went the broadsides; "Damn anyone who won't damn John Jay. Damn anyone who won't stay up all night burning a candle in his window damning John Jay." Jay claimed that he could have traveled the entire coastline from town to town at night by the light of his burning effigies.

A constitutional crisis also erupted in the House of Representatives in 1796 when the House threatened not to appropriate the funds needed to implement the treaty and demanded of Washington all documents relating to the negotiation of the treaty. Washington refused, arguing [that] the House had no power either to ask for such documents or not to appropriate the funds, that the treaty-making power was vested totally in the Senate, and if the Senate had agreed to the treaty, the House must appropriate the funds to put the treaty into effect—interesting argument. The House agreed to appropriate the funds by a vote of 51 to 48—quite close. What were the reasons? British abandonment of the Northwest Posts won over many westerners, and by this time, a very favorable treaty with Spain had been negotiated as a result of the Jay Treaty, something I will explain in greater depth in the next lecture.

Jay's Treaty, in addition to this constitutional crisis with the House, had four additional major consequences. First, the treaty is the single most important event in the formation of two national political parties. The first, known as the Federalists—taking their name from the group in favor of ratification of the Constitution—is led by George Washington, John Adams, and Alexander Hamilton and is identified as being pro-British. The other party becomes known as the Democratic-Republican Party and is led by Thomas Jefferson and James Madison, and it is identified as being pro-French.

As this lecture has shown, Jay's Treaty is far, far from the only issue involved here. You have deep domestic divisions and philosophical divisions. But what the treaty and the ratification struggle do is establish in the public mind the key stereotypes, symbols, and emotional appeals of each party—most importantly, the association of the Federalists with a conservative point of view and a pro-British policy in the European wars and the Republicans with a liberal point of view and a pro-French policy.

That is far, however, from the only consequence of the Jay Treaty. As previously noted, it will also lead to a major and highly favorable treaty with Spain, a treaty known as Pinckney's Treaty, in 1795. The terms of the Jay Treaty were not at first made public, and when the American envoy [Thomas] Pinckney arrived in Madrid, the Spanish concluded this was a treaty of alliance. They were about to leave the alliance with Great Britain, and they feared a joint Anglo-American attack upon their possessions and saw the need to mend fences with the United States.

The third result of the Jay Treaty was one of the most famous documents in this course, Washington's Farewell Address in 1796. The uproar caused by the treaty and the ratification struggle did not lead Washington to write the Farewell Address; as we will see,

Washington had had in mind writing a Farewell Address since 1792, but the foreign policy sections of the Farewell Address relate directly to the struggle over Jay's Treaty. Indeed, they are a consequence of Jay's Treaty, the struggle over Jay's Treaty, as well as Pinckney's Treaty, the Genêt affair, and everything that Washington had experienced in foreign affairs. They are also a defense of his policies, for Washington now came under assault as a tool of Hamilton and a tool of Great Britain and felt a need to defend himself.

Finally, Jay's Treaty would lead to an undeclared war with France, the so-called Quasi War, the naval war that would occur in the ensuing presidency of John Adams, and a near civil war in the United States from 1798 to 1800. We all look at the actual Civil War that did occur in 1861; there was a near civil war from 1798 to 1800, resulting from these divisions that we have gone through in this lecture and resulting from the fact that France, as well as Spain, considered Jay's Treaty to be a treaty of alliance. But where Spain was weak and tried to mend relations with the United States, France did the exact opposite. It responded violently and insultingly to the United States and faced a very forceful American response that, in turn, split the country.

In the next lecture, we shall explore all of these consequences of the Jay Treaty between 1795 and 1800 and one of the largest crises of the young infant United States.

Lecture Four

From the Farewell Address to the Quasi War

Scope:

This lecture begins with an explanation of what Washington actually meant in his famous Farewell Address, then explores one of the most important but often ignored periods in U.S. history: the 1797–1801 presidency of Washington's successor, John Adams (1735–1826). Washington's previous policies made possible a decade of peace with Britain and Spain but led to a serious deterioration in relations with the French. Adams attempted to resolve Franco-American disagreements but was unsuccessful; the results were the notorious XYZ Affair and an undeclared naval war between the two nations. That conflict, in turn, threatened to become a full-scale, declared war and to ignite a civil war in the United States. That neither event occurred can be credited to the courage of Adams, who defied leaders of his own Federalist Party in order to obtain peace with France and an end to the Franco-American alliance by 1800. The ensuing Federalist split resulted in Adams's defeat for reelection at the hands of the opposition leader, Thomas Jefferson, and thus, ended his political career.

Outline

I. As previously mentioned, Jay's Treaty had significant additional consequences for the United States, including spawning a major treaty with Spain, Washington's Farewell Address, an undeclared war with France, and a near civil war by decade's end. This lecture will explore each of these results individually.

II. The major positive consequence of Jay's Treaty—aside from the previously mentioned decade of peace with England and the opening of the Northwest to American settlement—was Pinckney's Treaty with Spain.

   A. At the same time that he sent Jay to London, Washington sent Thomas Pinckney (1750–1828) to Madrid to obtain free navigation of the Mississippi River, the right of deposit at New Orleans, and the 31st degree north latitude as the boundary of the United States with Spanish Florida.

B. By the time Pinckney arrived in Spain, the existence of the Jay Treaty was known, though not its specific contents. The Spanish feared that it was a formal alliance and would lead to combined Anglo-American military action against their New World possessions once they abandoned their alliance with England.

C. To prevent this outcome, the Spanish agreed in Pinckney's Treaty to everything the Americans desired: free navigation of the Mississippi River, the right of deposit at New Orleans, and the 31st parallel as the boundary between the United States and Florida.

D. But Jay's Treaty had the opposite impact on the French. They, too, concluded that it was a formal treaty of alliance and felt betrayed by the Americans. They began to seize U.S. ships and suspended diplomatic relations.

III. By this time, Washington had decided not to seek a third term in the elections of 1796 and to publish a Farewell Address to the American people.

A. Destined to become one of the most famous documents in American history, that address is shrouded in myth. It was not a statement of isolationism and, indeed, never mentioned the word or the concept. Furthermore, it was not even a publicly delivered address; rather, it was printed in a Philadelphia newspaper. Nor was Washington its sole author; its foreign policy sections were co-authored by Hamilton.

B. Washington's basic theme concerned the dangers of domestic factions. He warned that such factions would threaten liberty, lead to constant agitation, and "open the door to foreign influence and corruption" and, thus, a loss of independence.

C. He then warned against emotional attachments or antipathies toward other nations, as well as permanent alliances, and recommended as little political connection as possible while extending commercial relations with other nations.

D. Washington had voiced many of these ideas previously, but in the context of 1796, the Farewell Address was clearly designed as a public defense of his policies and an attack on his pro-French critics. As such, it was also a partisan political document geared to the 1796 election.

E. Simultaneously, it was a warning by a foreign policy realist against partisanship and emotionalism in foreign affairs and a proposed blueprint for achieving independence from Europe and empire in the New World.

F. Future generations, however, would interpret the Farewell Address quite differently.

IV. As if to fulfill Washington's warning, the French encouraged voters to support Jefferson. When Adams won, they authorized the seizure of any American vessel carrying British goods and refused to receive the new U.S. minister sent by Washington to Paris. Adams thus inherited a diplomatic crisis that would lead to an undeclared war.

A. Adams attempted to avert war by sending three envoys to Paris to obtain a virtual Jay Treaty with France. But the result was the notorious XYZ Affair, in which the French foreign minister, Charles-Maurice de Talleyrand, demanded a bribe and a loan to open negotiations.

B. When news of this outrage became public, Adams and the Congress agreed to arm U.S. merchant ships and to implement additional military measures; the result was an undeclared naval conflict known as the Quasi War.

C. Adams and Congress also agreed to the passage of the notorious Alien and Sedition Acts directed against both immigrants and the Republican Party press, which they labeled as treasonous, and to the raising of a large army for possible use against the Republicans, as well as French and Spanish possessions in the New World.

D. Jefferson and Madison responded to this direct threat to civil liberties with the Virginia and Kentucky Resolutions, claiming the right of a state to nullify a federal law that it considered unconstitutional.

E. The country now teetered on the edge of both civil war and full-scale war with France.

V. The fact that no civil or international war ensued was primarily attributable to Adams's political courage.

    A. Stunned by the U.S. reaction and facing new problems as a result of a major naval defeat to the British in late 1798, the French repealed their decrees against U.S. shipping and made clear their desire for new envoys and peace.

    B. Adams responded positively to the French overtures because he did not want to lead a weak and divided country into war and because he loathed and feared Hamilton and the High Federalists. He refused to ask Congress for a declaration of war or to fill the ranks of the army Hamilton would lead. Instead, he sent a new commission to France and purged his cabinet when Hamilton's supporters attempted to block him.

    C. The resulting Convention of Mortefontaine in 1800 ended both the Quasi War and the French alliance of 1778. It also prevented a civil war. But it created a formal split in the Federalist Party when Hamilton publicly denounced Adams, leading to Jefferson's victory over Adams in the 1800 presidential election. As such, this diplomatic move ranks as one of the most profound and important acts of political courage in U.S. history.

VI. In the next lecture, we'll look at the reasons Napoleon agreed to the Convention of Mortefontaine and Jefferson's reaction to the dictator's attempts to re-create the French Empire in the New World.

Suggested Readings:

DeConde, *The Quasi War*.

Gilbert, *To the Farewell Address*.

Questions to Consider:

1. How do you account for the differences between the meaning of Washington's Farewell Address in the context of 1796 and the meaning Americans gave it in later years?

2. In light of his critical contributions, why is John Adams less revered and studied than the other Founders?

Lecture Four—Transcript

From the Farewell Address
to the Quasi War

Jay's Treaty—as I pointed out in the last lecture—was pivotal in the formation of national political parties. It also had numerous additional consequences: a major treaty with Spain, Washington's Farewell Address, an undeclared war with France, and a near civil war by decade's end. In this lecture, we will explore each of these consequences individually.

Let's turn first to the treaty with Spain. At the same time that John Jay was sent to London, Thomas Pinckney was sent to Spain to obtain free navigation of the Mississippi River, the right of deposit at New Orleans, and the 31st degree north latitude as the boundary between U.S. territory and Spanish Florida. Pinckney's ship was fortuitously delayed, and by the time he arrived, news of Jay's Treaty had leaked out—but not the specific contents. The Spanish believed, incorrectly, that it was a formal Anglo-American alliance. This they greatly feared. They were in alliance with Britain against France, but they were about to leave that alliance, and what the Spanish feared was an Anglo-American combined military action against their New World colonies. Spain, being weak, felt it could not stop such an Anglo-American assault. It was, therefore, time to mend fences with the United States in order to prevent such an attack from taking place. The result will be the Treaty of San Lorenzo, also known as Pinckney's Treaty, in which Spain essentially agreed to everything the United States wanted: free navigation of the Mississippi River, the right of deposit at New Orleans, and the 31st degree north latitude as the boundary between Spanish Florida and the United States.

Now, the French also concluded incorrectly that Jay's Treaty was a formal alliance between the United States and Great Britain, but unlike Spain, the French are strong. They feel betrayed. They feel that Jay's Treaty contradicts the Treaty of Alliance that the United States still had with France and that Americans have turned on them, and they respond by seizing American ships and suspending diplomatic relations with the United States.

At the same time that this is happening, Washington decides he will not seek a third term as president in 1796, and he decides to announce this fact within a Farewell Address to the American people. The resulting document was destined to become one of the most famous in all of U.S. history, but it is a document shrouded in myth and misunderstanding. First and foremost, it is not a statement of isolationism. It never mentions the word "isolationism." It never mentions the words "no entangling alliances," and it never deals with that concept. Furthermore, the Farewell Address is not even a publicly delivered address. It is a document printed in a Philadelphia newspaper, and Washington was not its sole author. Indeed, the first draft had been written by James Madison for Washington in 1792, when Washington first thought of retiring, and the famous foreign policy sections were co-authored by Washington and Alexander Hamilton in 1796.

If our understanding of the Farewell Address is to be accurate, what does it actually say? Of course, the key message that Washington wishes to make clear is that he will not run again. We tend to skip over this. This was utterly critical for the future of this country. Washington could have had as many terms as he wanted. This denial of power (not for the first time), this willingness to give up power, was critical. It established a two-term precedent for the presidency that would not be broken until Franklin Roosevelt ran for a third term in 1940. And then in the 1950s, the Congress would pass an amendment and the states would pass an amendment making sure that Franklin Roosevelt was the only president ever to serve more than two terms. Presidents are now constitutionally limited to two terms. That was not the case in 1796.

Beyond that, Washington wished to warn his fellow citizens of certain dangers, based on his experiences. His basic theme was the dangers of political parties, especially when based on geography. Such parties, he warned, would threaten liberty, would lead to constant agitation, and would "open the door to foreign influence and corruption"—and, thus, a loss of independence, as different parties would side with different foreign powers, giving those foreign powers influence within the country. Washington also told his countrymen to: "Observe good faith and justice toward all nations. Cultivate peace and harmony with all." But avoid at all costs what he referred to as "inveterate antipathies against particular nations and passionate attachments for others." In other words, avoid emotionalism in foreign affairs. "The nation which indulges towards another an habitual hatred or an habitual fondness is in some degree a slave." He also added: "There is no greater error than to expect or calculate upon real favors from nation to nation. It is an illusion."

The "great rule" for the United States, Washington continued, was to have as little political connection as possible with others while extending commercial relations with other nations. European interests, he argued, were different from American interests, and geography enabled the United States to pursue such a course. If it did, the United States would be able to remain at peace and to build up its strength to a point where it could defy the great powers of Europe. Washington also added that the nation should avoid permanent alliances and that they were not in the national interest, though temporary alliances were acceptable for extraordinary circumstance.

Now, Washington had actually voiced many of these ideas previously. Let me give you just one example. In December of 1795, he had written to Gouverneur Morris:

> My policy has been, and will continue to be … to be on friendly terms with, but independent of, all nations of the earth. To share in the broils of none. To fulfill our own engagements. To supply the wants and be the carriers for them all; being thoroughly convinced that it is our policy and interest to do so, and that nothing short of self-respect, and that justice which is essential to a national character, ought to involve us in war; for sure I am, if this country is preserved in tranquility 20 years longer, it may bid defiance, in a just cause, to any power whatsoever, such, in that time, will be its population, [its] wealth and [its] resource.

But in the context of 1796, Washington's Farewell Address was clearly designed to be a public defense of his policies as well, most notably, a defense of Jay's Treaty, for which he was being savagely attacked at that point, but also a defense of his policies in regard to the Genêt affair and in regard to Pinckney's Treaty. Implicitly then, it is an attack upon his critics, who he considered to be pro-French and without good reason to be pro-French. Since 1796 was also a presidential election year, and since political parties had formed, and you had two candidates for president—John Adams for the Federalists, who was, at that point, vice president, and Thomas Jefferson for the Democratic-Republicans—Washington's Farewell Address can also be viewed as a partisan political document geared to the 1796 election and geared to getting John Adams elected president. Simultaneously, it is a warning by a foreign policy realist—and Washington is a foreign policy realist—against partisanship and emotionalism in foreign policy. He provides a blueprint for achieving independence from Europe and empire in the New World. For future generations, however, the address would be interpreted quite differently, as we shall see.

As if to fulfill Washington's warning, the French minister to the United States encouraged people to vote for Jefferson [and] against Adams in the 1796 presidential election. When Adams won, the French government authorized the seizure of any U.S. vessel carrying British goods, and it refused to receive the new U.S. minister that Washington had sent to Paris. John Adams, when he is inaugurated president in March of 1797, thus inherits a diplomatic crisis. Like Washington, Adams seeks to avoid war. Washington had sent John Jay to London to avoid war; Adams now sends envoys to Paris in an effort to obtain a virtual Jay Treaty with the French. But the French foreign minister, Charles-Maurice Talleyrand, refuses to even see the three envoys. As they are about to leave, Talleyrand's representatives visit them and demand a bribe and a loan to open talks with the French government.

We have here the notorious XYZ Affair, XYZ being the letters to refer to the French agents. Again, contrary to mythology, the bribe was insulting, but it was not what killed the talks; it was the loan, because the loan would have ended the neutrality of the United States. But when the bribe became known in the United States, it led to a public uproar and an undeclared naval war—known as the Quasi War—with the French on the high seas.

The XYZ Affair also resulted in passage of four notorious acts, known as the Alien and the Sedition Acts, directed against both immigrants and the Republican Party press, immigrants and a party press that the Federalist majority labeled as treasonous. What you have emerging here are two factors: One is what is known as "nativism," a hatred and fear of immigrants, even though this is a nation of immigrants, and the other is an attempt to repress the opposition press before the election of 1800.

What did these acts do? One act extended the naturalization period to 14 years, meaning that recent immigrants who would vote Jeffersonian would not be able to vote. Two of the laws gave the president the power to imprison or deport suspected aliens in time of war or in time of peace. The Sedition Act outlawed any statements against the government that were false, malicious, or scandalous. Twenty-five people would be arrested under this law. Every one of them was a Democratic-Republican newspaper editor. One of the most notorious cases was that of Matthew Lyon, who was also a congressional representative from Vermont. He is jailed, and his constituents reelect him to Congress from jail.

The Federalist Congress also passes bills to create a large army. To have a navy to fight the French in a naval war makes sense. Why have a large army? Of what possible use could such an army be? There are two possible uses. If this undeclared naval war with France expands into a full-scale war, the United States High Federalists hope [that the nation] would align itself with Britain and attack French and Spanish possessions in the New World. But the Democratic-Republicans fear there is another goal here. For certain High Federalists, it may very well have been a second goal to use this new army to forcibly suppress the Republican opposition. You do not yet have a concept of a truly loyal opposition within this country. The Federalists view the Republicans as traitors, tools of France, whereas the Republicans view the Federalists as traitors, tools of England.

In this situation, Jefferson and Madison responded to what they perceived to be a direct threat to civil liberties with the Virginia and Kentucky Resolutions, asserting the right of an individual state to nullify a federal law that it considered unconstitutional. There was no effort made to go to the Supreme Court since that was dominated by the Federalists, and indeed, the Supreme Court justices were enforcing the Alien and the Sedition Acts. You have here the origins of what will become the southern doctrine of nullification leading up to the Civil War in 1861. But what we see is that the United States is teetering on the verge of civil war in the 1790s, combined with full-scale war against France. Neither took place. There was no civil war at this time. There was no full-scale war against France. Why? Primarily, it is due to the political courage of John Adams, one of the least known of the Founding Fathers. Washington, Jefferson, Madison—Adams often gets buried, but his political courage at this point is extraordinary. What took place here?

Stunned by the American reaction and facing new problems as a result of a major naval defeat to the British in late 1798, the French government repealed its decrees against U.S. shipping, while Talleyrand made clear his desire for new American envoys, an end to the Quasi War, and a peace treaty. President Adams responded positively. He did not want to lead a weak and divided country into war. In addition to that, Adams loathed and feared Alexander Hamilton, who would lead the new army and, supported by other High Federalists, might run rampant in the country. Adams, therefore, refused to ask Congress for a formal declaration of war, and he refused to fill the ranks of the new army that Hamilton was going to lead. Instead, he decided to send a new commission to France.

In an extraordinary series of events, his secretary of state, Timothy Pickering, a supporter of Alexander Hamilton, tried to block him and, indeed, delayed sending the envoys. Adams discovered this and asked for Pickering's resignation. When he could not get it, he fired Pickering, as well as other Hamilton supporters within his cabinet. The envoys arrived in France to discover that Napoleon had, by that point, taken power. Napoleon was quite willing to make peace, though not on as favorable terms as the previous French government had been willing to. Terms were reached. The Convention of Mortefontaine (or the Convention of 1800) was signed, and it ended both the Quasi War between the United States and France and the French alliance of 1778. The American envoys had originally desired French payment for claims by American citizens for the seizure of their ships. Napoleon said he would not pay. The American government assumed those claims. Napoleon, in turn, agreed to end the alliance of 1778, and the Quasi War ended.

Adams thus prevented full-scale war with France, and one might argue that he also prevented a civil war, but his behavior created a formal split within the Federalist Party. Hamilton, infuriated by Adams's behavior, now publicly denounced the president. The Federalist Party split right before the election of 1800, and that played a role in Thomas Jefferson's ensuing victory over John Adams in the presidential election of 1800. There was one kicker, however: The Constitution—as I had previously mentioned—did not allow for political parties. You had not a separate vote for president and vice president but a simple tallying of electoral votes. The highest number of votes became president; the second highest number of votes became vice president.

Well, in the election of 1796, that meant that the president and vice president came from different political parties. In the election of 1800, party discipline held, and every Democratic-Republican elector wound up casting one vote for Thomas Jefferson and one for his vice presidential nominee, Aaron Burr. The result was a tie; a tie is to be decided in the United States Congress, with each state casting one vote. It is a Federalist-dominated Congress, so the Federalists will have to choose which Republican becomes president. Many of them, believing their own rhetoric about Thomas Jefferson, figured they would vote for Burr. Burr was a scoundrel, they thought, whom they could work with. Jefferson, they feared as an ideologue. Many of them believed that he was the Antichrist. Hamilton and others argued against this. They argued that Burr was dangerous and that Jefferson should be the one chosen as president— and in the end, Jefferson was. This will play a role in the next lecture, as we will see, in the conspiracy of Aaron Burr, which took place during Jefferson's second term.

Getting back now to John Adams, what Adams had done was an extraordinary act of political courage. It was an act of political courage that ended his own political career, and he knew it.

> I will defend my missions to France [he wrote], as long as I have an eye to direct my hand or a finger to hold my pen. They are the most disinterested and meritorious actions of my life. I reflect upon them with so much satisfaction, that I desire no other inscription over my gravestone than: "Here lies John Adams, who took upon himself the responsibility of the peace with France in the year 1800."

Adams, I would argue, is the unsung hero of his generation for this self-sacrifice. Self-sacrifice was deeply embedded within his political philosophy, something that I think is most clearly expressed in a letter he wrote to his wife, Abigail. When she asked him, "Why do you constantly deal with politics? You don't really like it," he responded as follows:

> I must study politics and war that my sons may have the liberty to study mathematics and philosophy ... navigation,

commerce, and agriculture, in order to give their children a right to study painting, poetry, music … and porcelain.

With Adams's defeat in 1800 came the defeat of the Federalist Party, both for the presidential election and in Congress. The Federalist Party would never again control the presidency or Congress. It would become a minority opposition party, and it would totally disappear within two decades. But the Federalist Party was of critical importance to American survival during the 1790s and, I would argue, to America's eventual rise to world dominance. It was the Federalists who made the new national government under the Constitution viable. We tend to assume today that, of course, this new government was going to work. There was no such guarantee in this regard in 1789. The Federalists are responsible for that. Under Washington and Adams, the Federalists also prevented involvement by a weak nation in a European war that could have destroyed the country. It could have destroyed the country externally and—as we have seen—it could have destroyed the country internally. In the process of doing this, the Federalists established the basic principles of American diplomacy for the duration of that century, the next century, and through and up to the present day. Equally important and closely related, the Federalists established a realist perspective for the future conduct of American foreign relations, best summed up in Washington's Farewell Address and his warnings against emotional attachments and emotional antipathies toward other nations.

One major remaining question: Why did the military dictator Napoleon Bonaparte, now ruling France, agree to the Convention of 1800 (the Convention of Mortefontaine)? He is not exactly a peace-loving man. Napoleon, however, needed peace with the United States, for—at this point in time—he had decided to re-create the French Empire in the New World. At the same time that he is signing this peace treaty with the Americans, he is signing an armistice with the British and arranging for the transfer of Louisiana from Spain back to France. All of these events—as we are going to see in the next lecture—are linked.

In planning this, however, I think Napoleon would have been wise to read the warning of the French minister to the United States, Pierre Adet, four years earlier, in 1796. The Federalists had been attacking Jefferson as a tool of France. Cutting through this propaganda, this paranoia, and these popular stereotypes, Adet wrote home an assessment of Thomas Jefferson in the following words:

> Mr. Jefferson loves us because he detests England; he seeks rapprochement with us because he distrusts us less than Great Britain; but he would change, perhaps tomorrow, from a sentiment favorable to us, if tomorrow Great Britain should cease to inspire him with fears. Although Jefferson is the friend of liberty and science, although he is an admirer of the efforts we have made to cast off our shackles and to clear away the cloud of ignorance which weighs down the human race, Jefferson, I say, is an American, and as such, he cannot sincerely be our friend. An American is the born enemy of all the peoples of Europe.

These words, as Napoleon was about to learn, were prophetic, for when Jefferson heard of Spain's retrocession of Louisiana and New Orleans to France, he would propose that the United States marry itself to the British fleet and, if necessary, make war on the country that he had previously befriended. Jefferson was, indeed, an American. Perhaps it was indeed true that Americans were the born enemies, at least in that time, of all the peoples of Europe.

Lecture Five
Jefferson and the "Empire of Liberty"

Scope:

Thomas Jefferson's election to the presidency in 1800 would lead to a dramatic shift in U.S. foreign policy, and his ideas regarding landed expansion and its relationship to liberty would dominate domestic policy for more than a century. This lecture explores those ideas and Jefferson's greatest success in obtaining more land for the United States: The Louisiana Purchase more than doubled the size of the country in 1803. We will also examine Jefferson's numerous efforts to enlarge the nation even further through his expansive claims regarding the boundaries of the Louisiana Purchase, as well as the famous exploratory mission of Lewis and Clark.

Outline

I. Thomas Jefferson's election to the presidency would lead to a dramatic shift in U.S. foreign policy, one based on his overall political philosophy, as well as his foreign policy views.

   A. Key beliefs within that overall political philosophy included republicanism as the guarantor of liberty, an agrarian society as the one best designed to promote and maintain liberty, and a strict interpretation of the Constitution as the surest way to avoid centralized governmental tyranny.

   B. In foreign policy, Jefferson was, first and foremost, an intense nationalist who saw the United States as the haven of liberty and its republican experiment as the wave of the future for the entire world. In effect, he equated the national interests of the United States with the interests of human freedom and progress and, thus, can be considered the nation's first ideologue.

   C. Jefferson saw Great Britain as the most powerful and dangerous enemy of the United States. France was a useful counterweight and, in its republican phase, an ideological ally.

D. Jefferson was also a semi-pacifist who believed that war was irrational and who desired isolation from the quarrels of Europe. He realized that complete isolation was not possible, however, and believed that trade and economic coercion could provide rational alternatives to war.

E. He was a strong proponent of landed expansion across North America as a means of maintaining both an agrarian republic and independence from Europe.

F. As president, Jefferson's intense nationalism and desire for landed expansion and an "empire of liberty" would triumph over and negate his other beliefs—most notably, his pacifism, his strict interpretation of the Constitution, and his anti-British and pro-French positions.

II. Jefferson's great foreign policy triumph was the Louisiana Purchase, which more than doubled the size of the United States.

    A. American settlers had been moving into this Spanish territory ever since the 1795 Pinckney Treaty and by 1801, they outnumbered French and Spanish settlers. Jefferson believed that this movement would peacefully Americanize the area and eventually force a weak Spain to sell it.

    B. In 1800, however, Napoleon signed the Treaty of San Ildefonso with Spain, regaining Louisiana for France as part of an effort to reestablish a French Empire in the New World. Jefferson found this move threatening in two respects.

        1. Unlike the weak Spain, a strong France could stifle the process of Americanization in Louisiana.

        2. Further, three-eighths of all American produce now traveled down the Mississippi River and through New Orleans; a strong France in that port constituted a mortal threat to both expansion and existing U.S. territory. To make matters worse, the Spanish governor of Louisiana revoked the right of deposit in 1802 when the treaty with France was formalized.

    C. Jefferson sent emissaries to Paris with instructions to purchase New Orleans or get an expanded right of deposit. He further told them to approach the British for joint military action if France refused and blocked the Mississippi River.

D. Jefferson's emissaries found Napoleon interested in selling not merely New Orleans but all of Louisiana as a result of his frustrations in fighting a slave insurrection in Haiti and his military and financial worries in Europe.

E. The United States thus obtained 828,000 square miles and New Orleans itself for $15 million in one of the greatest land deals in history.

F. Jefferson realized that the purchase violated his strict interpretation of the Constitution and, at first, desired a constitutional amendment granting the power for such a purchase, but the cabinet persuaded him against such a time-consuming process.

G. Whether Jefferson was an astute diplomat or merely lucky remains a matter of historical dispute. What is clear is that he violated many of his cherished beliefs to fulfill his dream of a continental empire.

III. Jefferson would further violate his beliefs in his efforts to obtain the most extensive boundaries possible for the Louisiana Purchase.

A. He had planned what would become the Lewis and Clark expedition as a way to lay claim to the area as early as the 1780s, and he obtained congressional funding for that expedition before he even knew that Napoleon would sell the territory.

B. He also instructed Lewis and Clark to explore as far as the Pacific Coast, thereby establishing a claim to the Oregon Territory.

C. Jefferson further insisted that the Louisiana Purchase included West Florida and Texas, and he threatened an alliance with England as a means of forcing Spain to negotiate the sale of these two areas. He would fail in both efforts, but his attempts set the stage for later American acquisition.

IV. Jefferson's expansionism had numerous positive and negative consequences for the United States.

A. It more than doubled the size of the nation, made it one of the largest countries in the world, and provided abundant land for Jefferson's agrarian-republican utopia. It also meant that in all likelihood, no European-style balance of power would emerge in North America; instead, the United States would dominate the continent.

B. But to obtain this land, Jefferson was willing to act in a duplicitous manner, violate many of his beliefs, and set some dangerous precedents for the future. In the process, he also planted the seeds of extinction for Native American cultures and, ironically, provided the resources and the national power to make the United States the commercial and industrial leviathan that Hamilton desired.

Suggested Readings:

DeConde, *This Affair of Louisiana.*

Kaplan, *Thomas Jefferson.*

Tucker and Hendrickson, *Empire of Liberty.*

Questions to Consider:

1. To what extent did the Louisiana Purchase result from Jefferson's astute diplomacy as opposed to sheer luck, as his critics claim?

2. Was Jefferson's "empire of liberty" possible, or was it, in reality, an impossible combination of contradictory concepts; that is, can one have liberty with empire?

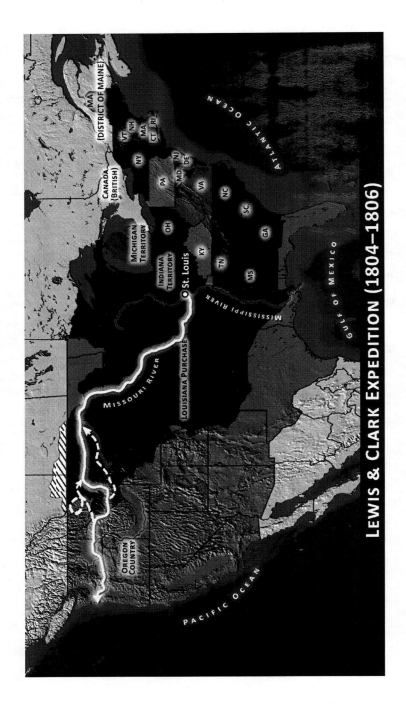

LEWIS & CLARK EXPEDITION (1804–1806)

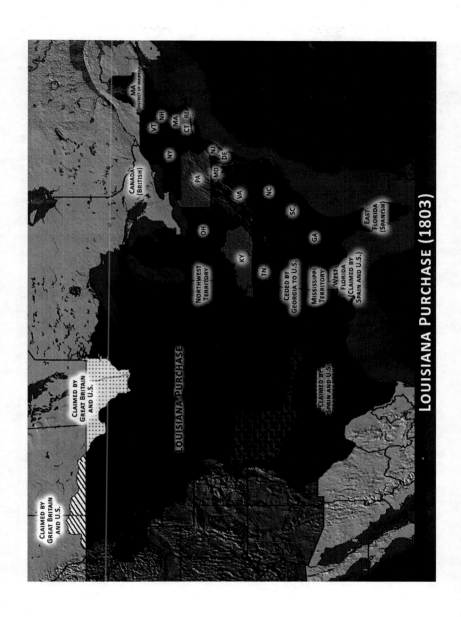

LOUISIANA PURCHASE (1803)

Lecture Five—Transcript
Jefferson and the "Empire of Liberty"

Thomas Jefferson's election in 1800 would lead to a dramatic shift in U.S. foreign policy, one based upon his overall political philosophy, as well as his foreign policy views. Jefferson is famous for his philosophy and for his intellect. President John Kennedy, in the early 1960s, invited the Nobel laureates to the White House and commented that the White House had not seen such an array of intellect and talent since Thomas Jefferson dined alone. That is obviously a gross overstatement. Jefferson, however, was an important philosophical thinker in terms of American history, and to understand his foreign policy, one must understand his political philosophy. He is a child of the Enlightenment, the 18th-century Enlightenment. He is a firm believer in rationalism and in progress. To him, one of the key components of progress, the key component in political affairs, is the concept of liberty. Liberty is the key human right, and representative government—republican government—is the guarantor of liberty.

Beyond this, Jefferson believed that an agrarian society was the one best designed to promote liberty and to maintain it. As he put it: "Those who labor in the earth are the chosen people of God." His belief in this regard was that self-sufficient farmers, [whom] he referred to as "yeoman farmers," were the epitome of independence. Within their daily labor, they were independent of others. They learned independence from their work, and they had a stake in society through their acquisition of property, and all of this would make them virtuous, independent citizens—the opposite would be those who lived in the cities. Urbanism bred dependence upon one another, and that would lead to tyranny. Jefferson also distrusted all forms of centralized power, which he viewed as tyrannical. He, therefore, insisted on a strict interpretation of the Constitution [and the] promotion of states' rights so as to avoid centralized governmental tyranny that could destroy liberty in the United States.

How do these views relate to his foreign policy views? Jefferson is, first and foremost, an intense nationalist. He sees the United States as the haven of liberty worldwide. Indeed, he sees the American republican experiment as the wave of the future for the entire world, and America's cause is, thus, the cause of liberty worldwide. In effect, what Jefferson is doing here is equating the national interests of the United States with the interests of human freedom and progress. He is considered by many to have been the nation's first ideologue in this regard.

Jefferson also believes that Great Britain is the most powerful and dangerous enemy that the United States faces. France serves as a useful counterweight and, in its republican phase, as an ideological ally. First, you had the American republican revolution, and then you had the French republican revolution—republicanism spreading around the world. But Jefferson had always considered the French Revolution to be secondary to the American Revolution, perhaps a bit inferior to the American Revolution. By the time he becomes president, the republican phase of the French Revolution has ended. Napoleon Bonaparte has established a dictatorship, and Jefferson is well aware that it is a dictatorship.

Jefferson is also a semi-pacifist; he believes that war is irrational and evil. I say "semi-pacifist," however, because—as we will see—he is willing to use force under certain circumstances, even though he does consider it irrational and evil. But the epitome of the warfare state is the entire European state system, and Jefferson, therefore, desires isolation from the quarrels and the wars of Europe. "I wish this nation," he wrote in 1785, "to be on the same footing with the world as China"—i.e., totally isolated.

In his first inaugural address in 1801, Jefferson referred to the United States as "kindly separated by nature and a wide ocean from the exterminating havoc of one-quarter of the globe"—i.e., Europe—[and its citizens] living in a "chosen country, with room enough for our descendants to the thousandth generation." It is Jefferson who used the term "no entangling alliances."

These views are not new. In 1799, he had written:

> I am for free commerce with all nations; political connection with none; and little or no diplomatic establishment. And I am not for linking ourselves by new treaties with the quarrels of Europe; entering that field of slaughter to preserve their balance. ... The first object of my heart is my own country. ... I have not one farthing of interest, nor one fibre of attachment out of it, but in proportion as they are more or less friendly to us.

But Jefferson realized that isolation similar to China's isolation was not possible. The quote about China that I cited from 1785 did not end with the comment "I wish this nation to be on the same footing with the world as China." Jefferson then went on to say, "[But] our people have a decided taste for navigation and commerce ... and their servants are in duty bound to calculate all measures on this datum."

We are not dealing here with New England merchants alone. Jefferson's own class, the Virginia planter class of the South, needed world markets for the staple crops that those plantations produced. Furthermore, his self-sufficient yeoman farmers did not wish to remain self-sufficient yeoman farmers. They wished to grow and sell a surplus, the same way he did. Indeed, many of them wished to become plantation slave owners, as he was a plantation slave owner.

There are two other facts to keep in mind: Jefferson believed that trade and economic coercion could provide rational alternatives to war for the nation—we saw that in the 1790s; we will see it again. And Jefferson was a very strong proponent of landed expansion across North America. He believed that such expansion would enable the United States to remain an agrarian republic, and he kept referring to the country as an "empire of liberty"; the more it grew, the more land it had, the more yeoman farmers it had, the greater its independence from Europe.

There were limits here. There were limits imposed by the technology of the times. This is pre-railroad. It is pre-rapid transportation, and there is literally no way to have a representative government that would cover the entire continent. How would the representatives from—let's say—Oregon get to Washington for a session of Congress? Their entire term of office would be spent traveling. Jefferson referred to the possibility of Americans moving west and, at some point, setting up "sister republics." Whatever the future was to be, the West was to be the key. As one scholar has pointed out, Jefferson saw the West in the same way that contemporary optimists see technology. It was the opportunity for constant renewal.

As president, Jefferson would find his beliefs in conflict with each other, and he would be forced to choose which beliefs were more important than others. Overall, I believe his intense nationalism and his desire for landed expansion and an "empire of liberty" would triumph over and negate his other beliefs—most notably, his semi-pacifism, his strict interpretation of the Constitution, and his anti-British and pro-French positions of the 1790s.

Jefferson's great foreign policy triumph was the Louisiana Purchase, which more than doubled the size of the United States. American settlers had been moving into this Spanish territory in large numbers ever since Pinckney's Treaty in 1795. By 1801, Americans in the territory outnumbered the French and the Spanish. Jefferson believed that this peaceful movement of American settlers into this territory would eventually Americanize the area and force a weak Spain to sell Louisiana to the United States.

But on October 1, 1800, Napoleon, in the secret Treaty of San Ildefonso with Spain, regained Louisiana for France. This was to be part of Napoleon's effort to reestablish a large French Empire in the New World. Louisiana was not Napoleon's focal point; present-day Haiti was. It was referred to then as the island of Hispaniola or Santo Domingo, and today, it constitutes Haiti and the Dominican Republic. This was the rich island that was to be the key to Napoleon's New World empire. Louisiana was to be its granary. It was to supply food to the people—the slaves, and the overseers, and workers on the island who were growing sugar and coffee on large plantations. The deal with Spain was that Spain would retrocede Louisiana back to France and give Napoleon six warships. In return, Napoleon would give a kingdom in Italy to the son-in-law of the Spanish king. The Spanish did attach a condition to this treaty, which was that Louisiana not be sold to a third party without the consent of Spain.

Napoleon realized that this treaty could lead to trouble with the United States and that the United States or Great Britain could seize the area in any war. He thus signed the Convention of Mortefontaine with the United States one day before the Treaty of San Ildefonso. He also signed a preliminary peace with the British on the same day as San Ildefonso. He planned out his moves carefully.

San Ildefonso was to be a secret treaty, but word of it leaked out. Jefferson found it extremely threatening for two reasons. First, unlike the weak Spain, the very strong France could stifle the process of Americanization in Louisiana. Furthermore, a strong France in New Orleans constituted a mortal threat, not simply to American expansion but to existing U.S. territory. Jefferson would note that already at this time, three-eighths of all American produce went down the Mississippi River system and through the port of New Orleans. You could not allow a strong, threatening power to control New Orleans. Jefferson also feared that the next time Britain and France went to war, Britain might seize the port of New Orleans, which would be just as dangerous as having the French at the port.

To compound the threat, in October of 1802, the Spanish governor in New Orleans revoked the right of deposit preparatory to giving the territory over to France. That decision was reversed in April of 1803, but the damage had been done by that point and Jefferson had acted. Jefferson and his secretary of state, James Madison, had first sent Robert Livingston as the new U.S. minister to Paris. Now, they sent James Monroe to join Livingston and with instructions to purchase New Orleans and/or portions of West Florida for $10 million or, at the very least, to get an expanded right of deposit at New Orleans. Jefferson further told Livingston and Monroe to approach the British for joint military action if France refused and if France blockaded the Mississippi River. As he wrote to Livingston on April 18, 1802, France had been "our *natural friend*," but:

> [T]here is on the globe one single spot, the possessor of which is our natural and habitual enemy. It is New Orleans … The day that France takes possession of New Orleans … fixes the sentence which is to restrain her forever within her low water mark. It seals the union of two nations, who in conjunction can maintain exclusive possession of the ocean. From that moment we must marry ourselves to the British fleet and nation.

Pierre Adet's 1796 warning, cited in the last lecture, had come true—or had it? Historical disagreement continues today as to whether Jefferson was serious or just bluffing. Jefferson knew that the carrier of this letter would inform the French government. Furthermore, he made no conscious move toward alliance with Britain at this time. Nevertheless, I think he was serious. I think we have to look at his statements combined with his other actions at this time. He ordered the acquisition of all possible Indian lands east of the Mississippi River. He issued warnings, and Madison, his secretary of state, issued warnings to the French minister to the United States and to Paris. Congress granted him the authority to call up 80,000 state militia [forces]. Perhaps most notable, he requested funds from Congress for an exploratory mission across the North American continent. This would become the Lewis and Clark expedition, but he requested the funds before he had any idea that he could purchase the Louisiana Territory.

This was not to be merely an exploratory mission to examine the flora and fauna of the New World; this would be a mission to lay claim to North America. Nor was this idea new; in the 1780s, when he had been the minister to Paris, [Jefferson] had attempted to organize such a mission to travel across all of Russia, the Bering Straits, and down through North America. The Russians had, of course, blocked it. Furthermore, at this time, the American minister in Great Britain and Jefferson's cabinet both assert what will become known as the "no-transfer principle" in the Monroe Doctrine in 1823. That principle is enunciated two decades before the Monroe Doctrine: that the United States will not tolerate the transfer of a European colony from one European power to another.

Monroe arrived in Paris on April 12, 1803, to find that Napoleon, on April 11—the day before—had offered Livingston not just New Orleans but the whole Louisiana Territory for $15 million. Why? Essentially, it was due to the frustrations and losses that Napoleon had suffered in crushing a slave insurrection on the island under Toussaint Louverture. He had sent over 30,000 troops to crush this rebellion in Santo Domingo. The troops had been successful, but they had suffered a very high casualty rate—above 50 percent—yellow fever had hit, and a new slave rebellion had broken out. Napoleon lost thousands and thousands of men, including his own brother-in-law commanding the army. Louisiana was considered worthless without Haiti, and Napoleon had had it with Haiti—as he supposedly commented at the time in disgust: "Damn sugar, damn coffee, damn colonies."

There were also delays in the actual transfer of Louisiana and in getting his occupation army into New Orleans. It was frozen in in European ports by an early winter and could not get out. Also, there was a looming resumption of war in Europe, and for such a war, Napoleon needed money. Furthermore, in a war, either the United States or Britain could easily take Louisiana—New Orleans in particular and, with it, the rest of Louisiana. Selling it to the United States would keep it out of British hands and turn the United States into a friendly neutral instead of an enemy. Speed in the negotiations was necessary in order to preclude a British attack or Spanish objections. Remember, by the Treaty of San Ildefonso, Napoleon could not sell it to a third party without informing Spain. He did not inform Spain. Indeed, he only held Louisiana for 20 days.

Did Napoleon realize what he was doing? Yes. "They ask of me a town," he said, "and I give them an empire." What about future U.S. power in 200 to 300 years? His reply: "my foresight does not enhance such remote fears." He added, "I have just given to England a maritime rival that will sooner or later humble her pride." As a result, the United States would obtain 828,000 square miles, including New Orleans, for $15 million—one of the greatest land deals in history. That works out to $0.03 an acre.

There were some problems. The purchase violated the financial limits that had been set, $10 million, and it violated Jefferson's strict interpretation of the Constitution. Nowhere in the Constitution is the national government explicitly given the right to purchase territory. Jefferson wanted a constitutional amendment to grant the government that power, but his cabinet talked him out of such a time-consuming process on the grounds that by the time it was finished, Napoleon would probably change his mind. Jefferson, therefore, buried his constitutional scruples and sent the treaty to the Senate. The Senate agreed to the purchase by a vote of 24 to 7, with the Northwest Ordinances set as the pattern for settlement and statehood.

Whether Jefferson was an astute diplomat or merely lucky remains a matter of historical dispute—to his supporters, [there was] brilliant diplomacy here; to his detractors, sheer luck. What is clear is that Jefferson violated some of his cherished beliefs in order to fulfill his dream of a continental "empire of liberty." He would further violate his beliefs in his efforts to obtain the most extensive boundaries possible for the Louisiana Purchase, something that Talleyrand predicted would take place when he commented to Livingston and Monroe: "[Gentlemen] you have made a noble bargain for yourselves, and I suppose you will make the most of it." That is exactly what Jefferson now attempted.

As I previously mentioned, Jefferson had planned what would become the Lewis and Clark expedition as a way to lay claim to the area. He had started planning it as early as the 1780s and had obtained congressional funding before he even knew that Napoleon would sell it. He now instructed Lewis and Clark to explore all the way to the Pacific Coast. They were thereby establishing a claim to the Oregon Territory, clearly not a part of the Louisiana Purchase. Their mission, running [from] 1804 through 1806, would do exactly that. You also had exploratory missions by Zebulon Pike, both in the North and in the Southwest area, where Jefferson would wind up claiming that Texas was part of the Louisiana Purchase. He would also claim that West Florida was part of the Louisiana Purchase.

As with the original purchase, Jefferson threatened alliance with England and war as a means of forcing Spain to negotiate for a purchase of West Florida and, perhaps, of Texas. At one point, he tried to take up Napoleon's hint of a bribe to Napoleon so that Napoleon would force the Spanish to sell West Florida to the United States. That effort failed, and so did the efforts to acquire Texas, but they would set the stage for later American acquisition of both territories. I'll spend a few moments on each of these—Florida first.

In 1808, Napoleon took over Spain. Two years later, in West Florida, American settlers revolted against the Spanish and proclaimed the Republic of West Florida. It was rather a comedy against 28 unarmed Spanish soldiers. In 1811, Jefferson's successor as president, James Madison, claimed the territory, and during the War of 1812, he took Mobile Bay and West Florida up to the Perdido River. The rest of Florida was obtained in the 1819 Adams-Onís Transcontinental Treaty, which we will explore in a few lectures.

The Texas claim became involved in what is known as the conspiracy of Aaron Burr. It was a conspiracy, we think, to create a private empire in the area. What was actually planned is still unclear, because Burr told different stories to different people. Very briefly, however, go back to the election of 1800 and the question of whether Jefferson or Burr would be chosen by the Federalists in Congress to be the next president. In the aftermath of this episode, Burr neither pushed for this nor denied that he would take the presidency; he just let events play out.

Obviously, trust between Jefferson and Burr, if it had existed, was broken at that moment. It was clear that although Burr was the vice president, he would not be Jefferson's running mate in the 1804 election. To recoup his political fortunes, Burr decided to run for governor of New York. Alexander Hamilton publicly denounced him and insulted him. Burr lost the race, and due to the insult, he challenged Hamilton to a duel. Dueling was illegal. They rode across the Hudson River and—in one of the most famous or infamous duels in all of American history—in Weehawken, New Jersey, Burr killed Hamilton. He was, at this point, a fugitive. "In New York," he wrote to his son-in-law, "I am to be disfranchised, and in New Jersey hanged. Having substantial objections to both, I shall not, for the present, hazard either, but shall seek another country"—one, it turns out, of his own making.

A conspiracy was launched with General James Wilkinson, our old friend, who was still in Spanish pay and now the governor of the Louisiana Territory. Again, there are different stories told to different people. In all likelihood, the conspiracy was to carve out a private empire composed of both Spanish territory and U.S. territory. As the plot became known, Wilkinson decided to betray Burr. His logic: "Perhaps, if I stay with Burr, I lose my Spanish pension, and I'm only second in command. If I betray Burr, I can keep my Spanish pension and remain a commanding general in the United States Army and look like a hero, and I will never be found out."

Again, we don't know the truth. We do know that Jefferson responded to rumors of the conspiracy with martial law and some extraordinary violations of civil liberties, including the arrest and prejudging of Burr as guilty of treason before his trial. The trial was presided over by none other than the chief justice of the United States Supreme Court, John Marshall, who reversed the ruling he had made two weeks earlier on the technical definition of treason so as to allow Burr to go free by coming up with a very narrow definition of treason. Why did he do this? Marshall hated and feared both Jefferson and Burr, and he probably felt at that moment that Jefferson was the greater threat.

Jefferson's claims and attempts to purchase Texas would be the first of many such attempts and would culminate in the 1836 revolt by American settlers, the annexation of Texas to the United States in 1845, and the ensuing war with Mexico. Jefferson's expansionism had numerous positive and negative consequences to the United States. It more than doubled the size of the country. It made the United States one of the largest countries in the world, and it provided abundant land for Jefferson's agrarian-republican utopia. It also meant that, in all likelihood, no European-style balance of power would emerge in North America; instead, the United States would dominate the continent.

But to obtain all this land, Jefferson had been willing to act in a duplicitous manner, to violate many of his beliefs, and to set some very dangerous precedents for the future. In the process, as some historians have noted, he also planted the "seeds of extinction" for Native American cultures, insisting that the Native Americans become agrarians and assimilate or be banished to the trans-Mississippi West. Furthermore, what would expand into this land were not only Jefferson's yeoman farmers and liberty but also slavery. Ironically, the Louisiana Purchase would provide the resources and the national power to make the United States the commercial and industrial leviathan of the world—a commercial and industrial leviathan that Hamilton had desired, not Thomas Jefferson.

Lecture Six
The "Second War for Independence"

Scope:

In addition to desiring landed expansion in North America, Jefferson and his followers strongly believed in the ability of peaceful economic coercion to obtain their foreign policy goals without resort to war and, thereby, the remaking of the rules of international relations. This belief was sorely tested between 1806 and 1812, as both Jefferson and his successor, James Madison, attempted to halt British and French wartime violations of American neutral rights through a series of economic retaliatory acts against the two powers. The failure of those acts, combined with a perceived British-Native American threat in the Northwest, led the United States into a second war with England in 1812. Although that war began disastrously for the Americans and is often considered a stalemate at best, it actually resulted in numerous gains for the United States—most notably, added security and British/European respect. This lecture concludes with an explanation of those gains and why the War of 1812 is often referred to as the Second American War for Independence.

Outline

I. In 1803, war resumed in Europe. By 1806, France, under Napoleon, was supreme on land, while Britain remained supreme at sea. The ensuing stalemate led both powers to practice economic warfare that would deeply affect the United States and lead it to war against Britain by 1812.

    A. Complaints against Britain focused on its impressment of seamen from U.S. merchant ships, its broad definition of contraband liable to seizure, its mid-ocean or "paper" blockades, and its so-called Rule of 1756.

    B. Although Britain justified these moves as war measures, Americans saw them as primarily designed to destroy a commercial rival that had become the largest neutral carrier in the world.

C. Napoleon retaliated with his Continental System, a series of decrees that not only closed Europe to British ships and goods but also made liable to seizure any neutral ship stopping in Britain or submitting to British customs or inspection.

D. As a result, U.S. ships could not trade with Europe without being subject to seizure by one side or the other.

II. Jefferson had long believed that the British were more of a threat to the United States than the French and that commercial retaliation could force concessions without resort to war; as president, he would practice such a policy.

A. He would do so with a new belligerency, one that illustrated militant opposition to any attacks on U.S. sovereignty and honor.

B. In 1807, the *Chesapeake*, one of the U.S. warships bound for the Barbary conflicts, was attacked and boarded by a British warship searching for deserters.

C. In response, Jefferson called Congress into special session and requested an embargo on all U.S. exports and shipping. His goals were to stop the ship seizures of both powers, issue a war warning to the British, and provide time to prepare for war if necessary; at the same time, he sought to use such economic coercion as a possible alternative to war. Gradually, this use of economic pressure became his great experiment and his great failure.

1. Jefferson believed that Britain needed U.S. goods more than the United States needed British goods and that the embargo would force British and French concessions without resort to war. But it actually complemented Napoleon's Continental System and hurt the American economy more than the British economy.

2. The embargo also led to massive opposition and smuggling in Federalist New England, to which Jefferson responded with coercive measures that violated civil liberties and expanded national power as much as war would have done.

3. Ironically, the embargo promoted manufacturing that Jefferson had previously opposed.

4. It also led to great gains for the Federalist Party in the 1808 elections and split the Republicans into warring factions.

III. James Madison, Jefferson's successor as president, would also attempt economic coercion, but in June of 1812, he gave up on this policy in favor of war.

A. Madison cited four issues in his war message, three of which concerned neutral rights: impressment, which was an assault on U.S. sovereignty; British naval acts off the U.S. coastline and paper blockades on the high seas; and the Orders in Council, which he argued were primarily designed to destroy U.S. commercial competition.

B. The fourth issue was British support for the efforts of Shawnee leader Tecumseh in the Old Northwest to block further American expansion by forming a confederation of all Native American tribes along the western frontier.

C. Supported if not pressured by a group of new, young, and highly nationalistic Republican congressmen known as the War Hawks, Madison argued that these British acts amounted to war against the United States.

D. Congress deliberated for 17 days before agreeing to war. It did so by close votes in both houses, with sharp splits along both sectional and party lines. Overall, the Republicans, who were dominant in the South and West, supported war, while the Federalists, who were dominant in New England, opposed it.

IV. The War of 1812 contradicts the cliché that the United States always wins the war but loses the peace.

A. Militarily, the nation almost lost the war, and at best, it achieved a stalemate by 1814.

B. Diplomatically, it also appeared to achieve a stalemate. In the Treaty of Ghent that ended the war (within the context of the end of the Napoleonic Wars), the United States and Britain essentially agreed to return to the status quo ante bellum.

C. Nonetheless, this conclusion masks the enormous gains the United States obtained from the war effort and peace treaty.

1. The major Native American confederations in the Northwest and Southwest were militarily defeated and destroyed during the war, and the British abandoned their efforts to create a Native American buffer state in the Old Northwest.

2. The United States gained new respect from Britain and the other powers of Europe for its military efforts and was acknowledged as the major power in North America.

3. Conflicts over neutral rights disappeared with the end of the Anglo-French wars in Europe. The resulting European peace also ended American preoccupation with Europe and allowed the United States to concentrate on internal development and continental expansion.

4. The navy that the Federalists had created in the 1790s distinguished itself during the war and remained a potent force afterward. It served as the cutting edge of American commercial expansion through its numerous exploratory missions and treaties, most notably, with China and Japan.

5. The bilateral commissions established in the Treaty of Ghent to deal with remaining Anglo-American disputes were successful and set the stage for the Anglo-American entente that would be so important to U.S. diplomatic successes in the ensuing decade.

6. Continued Federalist opposition to the war led to the demise of this national political party and a period of one-party rule in the United States known as the "Era of Good Feelings." Although not entirely true to its name, the era was one of intense nationalism and optimism. In reality, it also transformed the republican experiment, as the Jeffersonian agrarian vision gave way to expanded commerce, manufacturing, and market values.

Suggested Readings:

Brown, *The Republic in Peril.*

Horsman, *The Causes of the War of 1812.*

Stagg, *Mr. Madison's War.*

Watts, *The Republic Reborn.*

Questions to Consider:

1. Why did the United States go to war with Great Britain in 1812? Could or should this war have been avoided?

2. Assess the numerous successes and failures of both Federalist foreign policies from 1789–1800 and Republican foreign policies from 1801–1816. In retrospect, which policies were more appropriate for the young nation?

Lecture Six—Transcript
The "Second War for Independence"

In 1803, war resumed in Europe. Jefferson's sardonic comment?

> Tremendous battle in Europe. How mighty this battle of lions and tigers! With what sensations should the common herd of cattle look on it? With no partialities, certainly. If they can so far worry one another as to destroy their power of tyrannizing, the one over the earth, the other over the waters, the world may yet enjoy peace, till they recruit again.

Jefferson believed that Britain and France would compete for America's favor in this war. He was dead wrong. The exact opposite happened as both powers attacked U.S. commerce. By 1806, France, under Napoleon, was supreme on land. Britain, at the same time, was supreme on sea, particularly after the Battle of Trafalgar. The result was a military stalemate that led both powers to practice economic warfare against each other and against the United States. America thus had complaints against both powers. What were they?

Complaints against Britain centered on the so-called Orders in Council, decrees by the British government establishing a blockade not only against specific French ports but against all European ports controlled by Napoleon. By the rules of international law, you had to blockade a specific port, and not even the British fleet could blockade all of these ports. So what it did was to establish a blockade in mid-ocean, simply to stop any ships going toward Europe—not only in mid-ocean but also off the U.S. coastline, what the Americans would label "paper" blockades, which they argued, were illegal.

The British also defined contraband liable to seizure in very broad terms—not just guns and ammunition but clothing, food, and anything that could be used in war. They also began to enforce what they referred to as Rule of 1756, which was, again, simply a decree stating that any trade that was illegal in time of peace via mercantilist restrictions, the British would consider illegal in time of war, and they would seize neutral ships violating this rule. For example, if during a time of peace, no neutral ships could trade between the French West Indies and France (the so-called "carrying trade"), but in war, the French said to the American merchant fleet, "Of course, you can carry the goods for us," the British said that those ships are liable to be seized.

On top of all these issues, the British also impressed seamen from U.S. merchant ships. They would forcibly board U.S. merchant ships, seize seamen, and impress them into the British navy. Why did they do this? For one, the British navy needed manpower. Secondly, conditions in the British fleet were anything but good, and there were massive desertions into the American merchant fleet, which was expanding enormously at that point to take over the carrying trade. Conditions on U.S. merchant ships and pay were far, far better than they were in the British navy. The British would claim 20,000 desertions by the year 1812.

To make matters worse, if you did desert from a British ship, it was very easy to buy papers in the United States saying that you had been born in this country. It cost about $1 to do so. Furthermore, American courts were not likely to agree that the person had bought fraudulent papers. They were likely to agree that this was an American citizen.

But in addition to impressing their own subjects, the British also impressed numerous bona fide American citizens. The United States would claim 6,000 of these after 1803. This was an extremely emotional issue and a very important one to Thomas Jefferson. Indeed, he rejected what was, in effect, a new Jay Treaty with Britain in 1806, a treaty negotiated by James Monroe and William Pinckney, because it did not really deal with the impressment issue. What was so important to Jefferson about the impressment issue?

The British practice of boarding American merchant ships and forcibly seizing people from those ships violated U.S. sovereignty, it violated U.S. pride, and it violated the entire U.S. concept of citizenship. The Americans claimed you became a citizen by applying for citizenship. This was a nation of immigrants. The British claimed what was known as the concept of "indelible allegiance"—once an Englishman, always an Englishman. Acting on that principle, they were assaulting the very concept of American sovereignty and citizenship.

Britain justified most of its moves as war measures, but the Americans saw them as primarily designed to destroy the United States as a commercial rival, because the United States had become, by this time, the largest neutral carrier in the world. The U.S. re-export trade jumped from $13 million in 1803 to $36 million in 1804 and then up to $53 million by 1805.

Meanwhile, what is Napoleon doing? Napoleon retaliated against British measures with the so-called Continental System. In the Berlin Decree, he proclaimed a blockade of the British Isles. How do you blockade the British Isles if your fleet is at the bottom of the ocean and the British navy rules the high seas? He enforced the blockade by keeping all European ships in European ports and closing those ports to British ships and to British goods. Also, any ship carrying British goods or touching on British ports could be seized. The British responded by prohibiting neutral trade with the entire European continent unless the neutral ships stopped in England first and paid British customs. Napoleon responded to this with the Milan Decree, asserting that any ship traveling to England, submitting to British inspection, or paying British customs was liable to seizure. When you combine all of this, there is no way a U.S. ship could possibly trade with Europe without being subject to seizure by one side or the other. And by 1812, more than 800 U.S. merchant ships had been seized.

Jefferson had long believed that the British were more of a threat than the French, and he also noted that their assaults on U.S. shipping were occurring off the American coastline—not 3,000 miles away in Europe. Jefferson had also long believed that commercial retaliation could force concessions without resort to war. As president—as we will see—he would practice such a policy, but he would not limit himself to peaceful commercial measures. Indeed, there is, in Jefferson's presidency, a new belligerency to the man, one that illustrates quite clearly his militant opposition to any attacks on U.S. sovereignty and honor. He first exhibited these traits in response to the piracy and tribute demands of the Barbary States in the Mediterranean: Algiers, Tripoli, Tunis, and Morocco, [which]— if you remember from a previous lecture—had demanded tribute ransom from the United States and, indeed, from all powers. Jefferson, in the 1780s, had stated that he preferred war to the insult and expense of these continued tribute payments. And as president, he would send four different naval squadrons to the Mediterranean during his first term of office. He thereby initiated the overseas projection of U.S. naval force that would end tribute to the Barbary States by 1816. In fact, there is an extraordinary irony that the supposedly pacifist Thomas Jefferson projects U.S. naval force against the Barbary States during his tenure in office and establishes the U.S. Military Academy at West Point to train army officers, but that is another story.

The overseas projection of U.S. naval force became a hallmark of U.S. foreign policy, and it ties into the conflict with Britain because one of the warships bound for these Mediterranean conflicts, the USS *Chesapeake*, was attacked off the Virginia coast by the British warship *Leopard*. It fired upon the American vessel, and it boarded the American vessel; it was searching for deserters on June 22, 1807. It took four whom it claimed were deserters and then left.

This attack on the *Chesapeake* was different from previous attacks. Previous attacks had been on U.S. merchant ships. This was an attack on a U.S. warship, a ship of the U.S. Navy. That is an act of war, and it was one in which American sailors were killed and wounded. Jefferson called Congress into special session, but he did not request war. What he did request instead was an embargo on all U.S. exports and on all U.S. shipping, a complete shutdown on American shipping. Why? [First,] to stop the ship seizures of both sides. [Second,] to issue a war warning to the British. An embargo is a clear war warning. [Third,] to provide the time necessary to prepare for war, if necessary. The United States is not prepared for war at this time. [Fourth,] to simultaneously reassert his old idea of using such economic coercion as a possible alternative to war. Gradually, this becomes Jefferson's foremost reason, and the embargo [becomes] his great experiment in economic coercion. It is an experiment that fails, and it is his greatest failure as president.

Why did Jefferson do this? Why did the experiment fail? Jefferson believed that Britain needed U.S. goods more than the U.S. needed British goods and that an embargo would force British and French concessions without resort to war. It didn't work. As for the French, [the embargo] actually complemented Napoleon's Continental System. It helped the blockade of England. Jefferson realized that this could be the case, but he accepted that possibility because of his belief that Britain was the greater threat in that, as he put it, "Their naval tyranny is more bearing on us in every point of honor or interest."

But Jefferson overrated the importance of U.S. food and U.S. cotton to Great Britain, and he failed to understand Britain's wartime mentality. The embargo to Britain was a nuisance; Napoleon was a mortal threat. If Britain agreed to American demands, if it buckled under to the embargo, it would look weak to the nations of Europe, whom it wanted to re-gather into a new coalition against Napoleon. The British, therefore, would not give in—felt they could not give in.

Furthermore, the embargo wound up hurting the American economy more than it hurt the British economy. There was a deep economic depression in the country, especially in the South and West, and it led to massive opposition and smuggling, though ironically, not in the South and West, which continued to support Jefferson, but in Federalist New England. Smuggling along the coastline and smuggling across the Canadian border [took place]. Jefferson responded with a series of coercive measures that violated civil liberties and expanded national power almost as much as war would have expanded national power.

Ironically, the embargo also wound up promoting in New England the manufacturing that Jefferson had previously opposed. What were the New England merchants supposed to do, with their ships rotting in harbor? They invested their funds in manufacturing. But clearly, there is trouble here. New England is in a state of virtual insurrection against the embargo. In the South and West, people are supporting it, but they are grumbling. In the election of 1808, although James Madison is elected as Jefferson's successor and although the Republicans retain control of Congress, the Federalists make major gains, and the Republican Party splits into warring factions.

Madison will also attempt economic coercion, albeit a milder form of economic coercion. First, there's the Non-Intercourse Bill—no trade with Britain or France but trade with everybody else. Then, when that fails, in 1810, Macon's Bill No. 2 repeals all the restrictive economic measures but gives the president the power to reinstate non-intercourse against one of the two powers if the other one is willing to come to terms with the United States. One historian sardonically remarked on the two that Madison's policy had shifted from blackmail to bribery. There were attempts to negotiate differences within these. At one point, with the so-called Erskin Agreement, it looked like the United States and Britain would come to terms, but that failed.

With regard to Macon's Bill No. 2, Napoleon saw a wonderful opportunity, and in the Cadore Letter, he agreed to repeal his restrictions on American trade if the United States would reinstitute non-intercourse against the British. He was, as usual, lying through his teeth, and he continued to seize U.S. ships. Some historians say Madison was completely fooled by Napoleon. Others say Madison knew what was happening and went along with it as a way of separating Britain from France and forcing the British into repealing their orders. The British did repeal their Orders in Council but too late. Word arrived of the repeal after Congress had declared war in response to Madison's request that it do so in June of 1812.

In his war message, Madison listed four issues. Three of these concerned neutral rights: impressment, which he labeled an assault on American sovereignty; British naval acts off the U.S. coastline and paper blockades on the high seas; and the Orders in Council, which he argued, were primarily designed not because of Britain's war effort against France but to destroy the commercial competition of the United States. The fourth reason was different—British support for the efforts of Shawnee Indian leader Tecumseh and his half-brother, the Prophet, which is the English version of his name— Tenskwatawa was his Shawnee name, which I have probably mispronounced. Tecumseh and his brother, in the Old Northwest, made efforts to block further American expansion by forming a confederation of all Indian tribes along the western frontier. Tecumseh is not only a great warrior, [but] he is one of the great Indian diplomats. He sees that the only way U.S. expansion is going to be stopped is if all the tribes can unite against the Americans, and he is able to organize just about all the tribes in the Northwest by 1811.

At that point, he goes south in an effort to get the southern tribes into his confederation, at which point, the governor of the Indiana Territory, William Henry Harrison, decides militarily to move against [the] confederation while [Tecumseh] is absent. The result is the Battle of Tippecanoe, in which the Indians—although they are winning—abandon the field. Harrison claims a victory. Claims fly of British support for the Indians, and war fever spreads throughout the West.

That war fever is encouraged by a group of new, young, and highly nationalistic congressmen. From the frontier area and from the South, they are known as the War Hawks. They are led by Henry Clay of Kentucky, and they argue that these British acts amount to war against the United States. Whether Madison was pressured by these people or actually used them and had, on his own, decided for war is unclear, but this is his fourth reason in asking for war. Congress would deliberate for 17 days before agreeing to war, and it did so by very close votes in both houses—79 to 49 in the House and 19 to 13 in the Senate. There was also strong support for simultaneous war against France. And within the war vote against Britain, there were sharp splits evident along both sectional and party lines. The closeness of the war vote, the length of time it took, and these splits have all led to numerous historical disputes. Why did the United States go to war? What did this war vote show?

Overall, what we see is that Republican representatives in both the House and Senate—dominant in the South and West—supported war, while Federalists—dominant in New England—opposed the war. The Republicans voted 98 in favor of war and 22 against war. Most of the negative Republican votes were of Republican representatives in the Northeast. The Federalists voted 40 against war—not one Federalist in favor of war. Of those 40 Federalist votes, 31 came from the Northeast. What does one make of this?

One interpretation that I'm particular fond of, known as the "party ideological interpretation," argues that the Republican Party saw the British attempting to humiliate and strangle the United States and, with it, the entire worldwide republican experiment. Federalist gains continued into the elections of 1810 and 1812 and showed that the effort was succeeding. Remember, the Federalists are perceived as tools of England at this time.

In effect, what the Republicans do is to equate the republic (i.e., the United States), their Republican Party, and republicanism as a worldwide movement—all three are equal. They concluded that all three were in deadly peril and that war was the only option left open to them, despite their theoretical opposition to war. Whatever the reason, the United States is at war by June of 1812.

There is an old cliché that the United States always wins the wars but loses the peace. The War of 1812 contradicts that notion; it is a myth. Militarily, the United States almost lost the war. It did, indeed, lose the war in 1812. All of its efforts to conquer Canada ended in humiliating defeats to British forces and to the Indian Confederation under Tecumseh. Indeed, Detroit surrendered—one of the most humiliating surrenders in American military history—and the entire frontier was rolled back.

In 1813, the Americans were a bit better but not that much better. In 1814, the Americans were forced to shift from offensive operations—to conquer Canada—to defense. The reason? Britain and its allies had, by that point, defeated Napoleon and, thus, Britain no longer had to fight the Americans with one hand tied behind its back. Given the danger that the British faced, I would argue [that] the British had been fighting not with one hand tied behind their backs but with 9 of their 10 fingers tied behind their backs

Now they are free, and they send large veteran armies and naval forces into North America. One is to march down the Champlain valley in a repeat of the British strategy from the War for Independence and to try to separate Federalist New England from the rest of the United States. Another force is to attack the Chesapeake Bay and then swing south and take New Orleans.

The British will succeed in Chesapeake Bay. The Americans suffer a humiliating defeat in front of Washington, DC, and the capital is burned by the British in retaliation for the previous American burning of York, the capital of Ontario, present-day Toronto. But in Baltimore, there is successful resistance to the British, and it is where "The Star-Spangled Banner" is written by Francis Scott Key, watching the assault on Baltimore.

The British assault down the Champlain valley to split New England fails when the British fleet is stopped on Lake Champlain by Captain Thomas MacDonough in the Battle of Plattsburg Bay—at which point, not having control of communications across Lake Champlain, the British Army retreats back into Canada. After the peace treaty was signed but before people knew that a peace treaty had been signed, General Andrew Jackson then turned back the British assault at New Orleans with a stupendous victory against the British.

These final American victories tended to mask in the American mind—and mask to this very day—the years of military defeat that had preceded these last victories. The best you can say is that the United States had achieved a military stalemate by 1814.

Diplomatically, the war also appeared to be a stalemate at best, as the two nations essentially agreed in the Treaty of Ghent that ended the war. It was signed on Christmas Eve and within the context of the end of the Napoleonic Wars. But in that Treaty of Ghent, the two sides essentially agreed to return to the status quo ante bellum, to the way things had existed before the war—not exactly a U.S. victory.

By the way, the American negotiating team at Ghent was quite interesting. Secretary of the Treasury Albert Gallatin headed it, but within that team were two of the rising stars in American politics, representing the new generation of leadership in the country. Henry Clay, the War Hawk, is placed on the negotiating team, and John Quincy Adams, the Massachusetts son of John Adams, is also placed on the negotiating team. The two of them argue quite a bit. Indeed, their arguments over the terms of the treaty are almost as fierce as the arguments with the British, with Gallatin playing the peacemaker. Adams was representing the interests of New England, and Clay, the interests of the West. Personality-wise, they were exact opposites. A famous story is told of Adams, the Puritan, waking up at about 4:00 in the morning to say his prayers and writing in his diary that on the staircase he meets Henry Clay coming up from a card game that had just broken up. The two of them would become political allies, with the two—both brilliant—clearly representing the new generation of leaders.

Was the Treaty of Ghent, though, really a stalemate? Technically, it seemed to show a stalemate, but I think it masked enormous gains that the United States actually obtained from the War of 1812 and from this peace treaty. For good reason, this war became known as the Second American War for Independence. What were these hidden gains? First, the major Indian confederations in both the Northwest and the Southwest are militarily defeated and destroyed during the war. Tecumseh is killed in the Battle of Thames River in 1813. In the Southwest, General Andrew Jackson defeats the Creek Confederation in the Battle of Horseshoe Bend in 1814 and forces upon them the Treaty of Fort Jackson, in which they are forced to cede huge chunks of land. British diplomats at Ghent abandoned previous efforts to create an Indian buffer state in the Northwest. The war was a disaster for the Indians. The entire frontier was opened to rapid white settlement.

There was also new respect from Britain and the other powers of Europe for American military efforts. The British writer Michael Scott would later write the following:

> I don't like Americans; I never did, and [I] never shall like them ... I have no wish to eat with them, drink with them, deal with, or consort with them in any way; but let me tell the whole truth, *nor fight* with them, were it not for the laurels to be acquired, by overcoming an enemy so brave, determined, and alert, and [in] every way so worthy of one's steel, as they have always proved.

Along with that respect came recognition of the United States as the major power in North America. Conflicts over neutral rights disappeared with the end of the Napoleonic Wars. Europe would not go into general war for a century, and the resulting peace also ended American preoccupation with Europe and allowed the nation to concentrate on internal development and continental expansion.

The navy that the Federalists had created in the 1790s and that Jefferson had used against the Barbary States distinguished itself during the war and remained a potent force thereafter. Indeed, it obtained favorable treaties, ending tribute with all the Barbary States by 1816, and would remain the cutting edge of American commercial expansion via numerous exploratory missions and treaties, most notably, with China and Japan in the 1840s and the 1850s.

Bilateral commissions established in the Treaty of Ghent dealt with a host of remaining Anglo-American disputes, and that set the stage for the Anglo-American entente that would be so important to U.S. diplomatic successes in the ensuing decade. Continuing Federalist opposition to the war, culminating in the Hartford Convention, led to their demise as a national political party and a period of one-party rule in the United States, known as the "Era of Good Feelings." The Federalists had continued to oppose the war and, ironically, became champions of states' rights in an effort to halt it. They called for a convention in Hartford in which they called for constitutional amendments in this regard and vaguely threatened secession. Immediately following was news of American military victories at Plattsburg Bay and New Orleans, plus the Treaty of Ghent. The Federalists appeared to be fools or traitors, and they disappeared within a few years.

While misnamed, the following "Era of Good Feelings" would be an era of intense nationalism and optimism, one based, at least partially, on the belief that the war had revitalized and reaffirmed the republican experiment. But in reality, it had also transformed that experiment, as Jefferson's agrarian vision gave way to expanded commerce, manufacturing, and market values to which we must now turn.

Lecture Seven
John Quincy Adams & American Continentalism

Scope:

The conclusion of the Anglo-French wars in Europe ended the assaults on American neutral rights and the ensuing American preoccupation with European affairs. It also opened the North American continent to further U.S. expansion. A vital component of that expansion was the brilliant diplomacy of John Quincy Adams, considered by many historians to have been America's greatest secretary of state. This lecture examines his continental vision for the United States and his numerous diplomatic achievements in support of that vision: the Transcontinental Treaty with Spain that gave Florida to the United States and a claim to the Pacific Coast, the series of critical treaties with Great Britain that settled outstanding Anglo-American territorial and commercial disputes and made the former enemies unofficial allies, and the resulting Monroe Doctrine that Adams wrote and that defined the entire Western Hemisphere as an area reserved for future U.S. expansion and influence.

Outline

I. John Quincy Adams (1767–1848) clearly ranks as one of the most important but least recognized early figures in the rise of the United States to superpower status.

   A. He was one of the first policymakers to visualize the United States expanding across the entire North American continent and was a strong proponent of commercial expansion overseas, thereby neatly fusing old Federalist with old Republican foreign policies.

   B. When he took over the State Department in 1817, he had already amassed a wealth of diplomatic and political experience as minister to the Netherlands, Prussia, Russia, and Britain, as well as senator from Massachusetts and negotiator at Ghent.

   C. As secretary of state from 1817 to 1824, Adams was responsible for a series of major territorial agreements with Great Britain and Spain that would give the United States the rest of Florida, as well as a major claim to the Oregon

Territory and the Pacific Coast. He was also the primary author of what became known as the Monroe Doctrine, and he is considered by many to have been the greatest secretary of state in U.S. history.

II. Adams believed that good relations with Britain were essential to his expansionist plans and quickly acted to negotiate a series of crucial Anglo-American agreements.

    A. Simultaneously, Britain began to recognize the importance of good relations with the United States in the aftermath of the Napoleonic Wars.

    B. After the Treaty of Ghent, Adams, then U.S. minister in London, negotiated a new commercial treaty with Britain in 1815 that included the most-favored-nation clause.

    C. In 1817, his overture led to the Rush-Bagot exchange of notes and the ensuing treaty that limited naval forces on the Great Lakes and Lake Champlain; this was the first reciprocal naval arms limitation treaty in modern history.

    D. The Boundary Convention of 1818 dealt with issues of trade, fishing rights, and slaves, as well as the boundary between the United States and British North America.

        1. It set the boundary at the 49th degree north latitude from the Lake of the Woods to the Rocky Mountains.

        2. It established joint occupation of the Oregon Territory when the two sides could not agree to a permanent division of the area.

        3. The United States obtained permanent fishing rights off the coast of Newfoundland and Labrador.

        4. The two nations agreed to Russian mediation of the American demand for compensation for slaves seized by the British during the War of 1812, a mediation that eventually led to Britain paying the United States $1.2 million.

        5. The treaty also renewed indefinitely the clauses of the 1815 commercial treaty, and in 1822, Britain partially opened the West Indies to U.S. ships.

E. Although by no means ending all disputes between the two nations, these agreements established cordial relations that freed Adams for more intense territorial negotiations with the Spanish and would eventually result in the Monroe Doctrine.

III. In the negotiations that would result in the Transcontinental Treaty of 1819, Adams desired to obtain the rest of Florida, Spanish agreement to the Louisiana Purchase and to boundaries that would include Texas, and removal of any Spanish claim to Oregon, without limiting his freedom of action to recognize the newly independent republics of Latin America.

A. Adams used General Andrew Jackson's seizure of East Florida in 1818 to break a deadlock in the negotiations and force Spain to accede to his wishes.

B. Consequently, the Spanish agreed to cede Florida to the United States in return for U.S. assumption of $5 million worth of old claims by its citizens against Spain and to a boundary between U.S. and Spanish territory that eliminated Spanish claims to Oregon and implicitly recognized U.S. claims there. In return, Adams gave up U.S. claims to Texas but retained full freedom of action in Latin America.

C. In 1822, after Spain finally ratified the treaty, the United States recognized the independence of the republics of Latin America.

IV. In the following year, Adams authored one of the most famous documents in American history: the Monroe Doctrine.

A. The doctrine originated as a response to Russian claims to the Pacific Coast down to 51 degrees north latitude, the suppression by the Holy Alliance of republican revolutions in Italy and Spain, and an ensuing fear of European reconquest in Latin America.

B. British Foreign Secretary George Canning similarly feared an effort by the Holy Alliance to reconquer Latin America and suggested a joint Anglo-American note warning the European powers against any such effort.

C. Adams convinced the cabinet and President James Monroe (1758–1831) to issue a unilateral statement, one that appeared in the president's annual message to Congress in late 1823 and that enunciated a series of major principles:

1. Non-colonization: The Western Hemisphere was no longer open to colonization by the Europeans.

2. Non-intervention: The two hemispheres constituted two distinct political and geographic areas, one ruled by monarchies and the other consisting of republics. The United States would oppose any effort to extend the European system to the New World.

3. Non-interference: In return for non-intervention, the United States would not interfere in the internal affairs of Europe.

4. No transfer (actually a corollary asserted separately but implicit within the doctrine): The United States would oppose the transfer of any existing colony in the Western Hemisphere from one European power to another.

D. Contrary to popular myth, the Monroe Doctrine had no legal status and was ignored by the European powers. What prevented European intervention in the New World at this time was not this bold assertion but, as Adams realized, London's refusal to tolerate such intervention and the power of the British fleet. For many decades, that fleet would, in effect, enforce the doctrine.

E. What Adams (and Monroe) had done was to assert a series of principles that essentially declared the entire Western Hemisphere to be a U.S. sphere of influence. The United States did not yet have the power to enforce these principles, but Adams realized that the British would enforce them in their own interests.

F. Adams and Monroe had, in effect, fulfilled Washington's prophecy in his Farewell Address: that given time and peace, the United States would be able to defy the powers of Europe.

G. Ironically, Adams later turned against the expansionism he had done so much to promote. He also warned Americans against going abroad on ideological crusades to remake the world, warnings that were clearly prescient.

Suggested Readings:

Bemis, *John Quincy Adams and the Foundations of American Foreign Policy.*

Dangerfield, *The Era of Good Feelings.*

Lewis, *John Quincy Adams.*

Weeks, *John Quincy Adams and American Global Empire.*

Questions to Consider:

1. Why was Adams able to achieve such extraordinary successes as secretary of state?

2. Is the Monroe Doctrine an assertion of an essentially defensive or an aggressive U.S. policy in the Western Hemisphere?

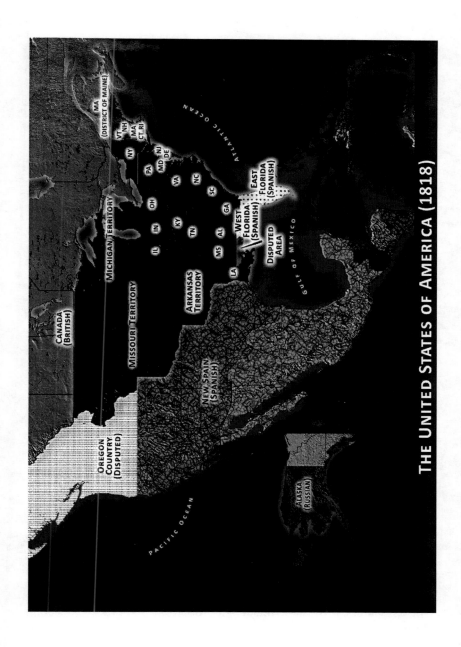

THE UNITED STATES OF AMERICA (1818)

Lecture Seven—Transcript
John Quincy Adams & American Continentalism

John Quincy Adams, whom we met in the last lecture, the son of John Adams, clearly ranks as one of the most important but least recognized early figures in America's rise to superpower status. Adams was one of the first policymakers to visualize the United States expanding as a single nation across the entire continent. Jefferson had his doubts and talked about sister republics, but you now have your transportation revolution in full force, with the steamboat and the railroad making possible the conception and the reality of the United States as a continental nation.

Simultaneously, Adams was a strong proponent of commercial expansion overseas. He thus fused the old Federalist beliefs in this regard with the old Republican foreign policy beliefs. That was quite appropriate, given the fact that he had begun as a Federalist and then shifted to Jefferson's Democratic-Republican Party. His enemies referred to him as an amphibian, one who moved on land and on sea.

In 1817, the new president, James Monroe, appointed Adams secretary of state. By that time, he had already amassed a wealth of diplomatic and political experience, including minister to the Netherlands, minister to Prussia, minister to Russia, minister to Great Britain, senator for Massachusetts, and one of the negotiators of the Treaty of Ghent, ending the War of 1812.

Like his father, however, John Quincy Adams was a difficult human being. As one historian put it: "He spent his life in the public service, for which he was peculiarly fitted, except in one respect—he was almost totally deficient in the art of getting on with other people." His self-assessment was no better: "I am," he wrote, "a man of reserved, cold, austere, and forbidding manners; my political adversaries say a gloomy misanthropist, and my personal enemies, an unsocial savage." Perhaps this is one reason why he is underrated and forgotten by most people. Another reason may be the fact that he had only a one-term presidency—it was a failed presidency—from 1825 to early 1829, under disputed circumstances, and he was defeated for reelection by none other than Andrew Jackson.

But as secretary of state under Monroe from 1817 to 1824, John Quincy Adams would be responsible for an extraordinary series of major foreign policy successes: territorial agreements with Britain and Spain that would give the United States the rest of Florida, as well as a major claim to the Oregon Territory and the Pacific Coast, and primary authorship of the Monroe Doctrine, which many argue should be called the Adams Doctrine. He is considered by many historians to have been the greatest secretary of state in U.S. history. Adams believed that good relations with Great Britain were now both possible and essential to his plans for continental expansion, and he quickly acted to negotiate a series of crucial Anglo-American agreements in the aftermath of the War of 1812.

The British simultaneously recognized the importance of good relations with the United States, primarily due to their recognition of the importance of the American market for their manufactured goods. The United States consumed one-sixth of all British manufactured goods, and the British realized this. As British Prime Minister Lord Liverpool put it:

> America is the one whose increasing population and immense territory furnish the best prospect for British produce and manufactures. Everybody, therefore, who wishes prosperity to England must wish prosperity to America.

Furthermore, in the decade following the defeat of Napoleon, Britain found itself engaged in major disagreements with her former continental allies and began to look for new allies overseas. The result was a growing entente, an understanding, between the two former enemies, London and Washington. Adams would play a key role in this. In the aftermath of the Treaty of Ghent, when Adams becomes the U.S. minister to London, he will negotiate a new commercial treaty with Great Britain that will include the most-favored-nation clause. Then, in 1817, his overture will lead to the Rush-Bagot Agreement, an exchange of notes that eventually become a treaty limiting naval forces on the Great Lakes and Lake Champlain.

Contrary to popular myth, this is not the beginning of the demilitarized border and the unguarded Canadian-American frontier. You have to wait many years before you get that. But it is the first reciprocal naval arms limitation treaty in modern history, and it was a major step in the eventual demilitarization of the Great Lakes system, the largest freshwater system in the world.

It was also an important early step in the Anglo-American entente, and it set the stage for the next step: the Anglo-American Boundary Convention of 1818. That boundary convention set the boundary between the United States and Canada at the 49th degree north latitude, from the Lake of the Woods in northern Minnesota to the Rocky Mountains. It also established joint occupation of the Oregon Territory. That is a territory stretching from the present boundary between California and Oregon all the way up to the boundary between British Columbia and Alaska. It is a territory that, at this point, is claimed by four countries: Spain, Russia, Britain, and the United States.

Adams attempted to negotiate a final settlement with the British, but the two sides could not agree to a permanent dividing line. The key conflict here is that the British wished to divide the Oregon Territory at the Columbia River, the present boundary between the state of Oregon and the state of Washington. Adams wanted the division to take place much farther north so as to include Puget Sound. He realized that the West Coast, unlike the East Coast, had very few natural harbors; Puget Sound was one of them. He realized—he had been told this by New England seamen—that the mouth of the Columbia River presented major problems. There was a major sandbar there, and it could not develop, and Puget Sound was more important.

That was not the limit of this treaty. It also dealt with a host of other Anglo-American issues, [including] permanent U.S. fishing rights off the coast of Newfoundland and Labrador [and] a mediation by Russia of an old U.S. demand for compensation for slaves seized during the War of 1812. The boundary convention also renewed indefinitely the clauses of the 1815 commercial treaty that Adams had negotiated, and in 1822, Britain would partially open the West Indies to U.S. ships.

This was by no means ending all the disputes between the United States and Great Britain, but all of these agreements did establish cordial Anglo-American relations that, in turn, freed Adams for more intense territorial negotiations with the Spanish. These would culminate in the Transcontinental, or Adams-Onís, Treaty of 1819. They would also eventually result in the Monroe Doctrine.

But let us first turn to the Transcontinental Treaty. Adams desired recognition from Spain of the Louisiana Purchase. He desired to purchase East Florida. He wanted boundaries to Louisiana that would include Texas, and he wanted to remove any Spanish claim to any part of the Oregon Territory. He wanted to obtain all of this without in any way limiting his own freedom of action to recognize the newly independent republics of Latin America when he felt like recognizing them. The Spanish minister to the United States, Don Luis de Onís, wanted to prevent just about all of this. Indeed, Onís had begun by arguing that the Louisiana Purchase itself was fraudulent. Obviously, there was no basis for talks. Negotiations continued, however, through 1817 and 1818. They were not getting anywhere very rapidly when the deadlock was broken in 1818 by an event known to some historians as "Andrew Jackson's 1818 rampage" through East Florida. What happened here?

Jackson had been placed in charge of an army that was chasing Indians and runaway slaves who had been crossing the border from Florida and taking refuge in Spanish territory. Jackson decided to ignore the international boundary. He invaded East Florida. He took the Spanish towns in St. Marks and Pensacola; deposed the Spanish governor (later stated that he regretted not hanging the man); seized the Spanish archives; appointed his own American governor; and then captured, tried, and executed two British subjects in the area, Alexander Arbuthnot and Robert Ambrister. As one historian has put it: "The trial of two British subjects before an American court in a fortress legally the property of Spain was a circumstance too complex for anyone ever to make any sense out of it."

Onís was enraged, and so was Monroe's cabinet. The cabinet wanted to disavow Jackson, while Onís demanded the return of territory, and indemnity, and punishment. But Adams convinced the cabinet not to disavow Jackson [but,] rather, to allow him to use this event to break the deadlock with Onís. How? He informed Onís that he would return the territory to Spain, but there would be no apology, there would be no indemnity, and there would be no punishment, that indeed, Jackson's invasion was justified by the Pinckney Treaty of 1795, which had contained a clause in which each side pledged to control the Indians on its side of the border. Spain had failed to do so, thereby granting the United States the right of defensive invasion—if you will, a preemptive attack. This was, Adams admitted, not an international law, but it was "the common sense of mankind." Cutting through that verbiage, what Adams was saying to Onís was: "Either you put in an adequate force to defend this area and control your Indians or cede it to us. And if the Indians raid again, we'll take it again, and this time, we probably won't give it back."

The Spanish were thereby forced to realize the hopelessness of their situation. Onís was instructed to give up East Florida and anything else he had to in order to get a secure boundary between U.S. territory and the Spanish Empire in Mexico and Central America. Onís thus agreed to cede East Florida to the United States in return for an American assumption of $5 million worth of old claims by its citizens against Spain. He also agreed to a step-by-step, staircase-type boundary between the Louisiana Territory and Spanish territory all the way to the Pacific Coast. In return, Adams gave up U.S. claims to Texas. He did not have to; Onís had the authority to give up this, as well. [Adams] did not have to, and he did not want to, but the rest of the cabinet said, "Don't push it; give that up to get everything else."

In addition to all these gains, Adams retained full freedom of action regarding the republics of Latin America. He could do what he wanted to, when he wanted to. To Adams, the most important thing about this treaty was the line to the Pacific Coast. It was everything to him, but in reality, it was nothing. There was no piece of land to which America held unquestioned title on the Pacific Coast. But Onís, by agreeing to this boundary line with the Americans, in effect, agreed to Spanish recognition that the Americans did have a claim north of the line. He had also gotten Britain to recognize that the United States had some claim, though at that point, it was simply joint occupation. Spanish claims to Oregon had been eliminated, while American claims had been implicitly recognized. Adams considered the signing day of the treaty as the most important day of his life. Spain would delay ratification of the treaty until 1822, but once the Spanish did ratify the treaty, Adams recognized the independence of the republics of Latin America.

In the following year, 1823, Adams authored one of the most famous documents in all of American history, the Monroe Doctrine. The Monroe Doctrine originated as a response to three events. The first [took the form of] Russian claims to the Pacific Coast all the way down to 51 degrees north latitude, part of the Oregon Territory, with a decree that no other ships were to be allowed within 100 miles of the coastline. Second [was] the suppression by Britain's former allies on the continent of Europe, the so-called Holy Alliance (Austria, Prussia, Russia, and now, once again, monarchial France), of republican and constitutional revolutions in Italy and in Spain. At the Congress of Verona in 1822, the continental powers had granted France permission to send an army into Spain to crush a constitutionalist movement and restore the Spanish king to full power. There was an ensuing fear that France and these other European allies would attempt to help Spain in the reconquest of Latin America.

The Americans were not the only ones to have such fears. British Foreign Secretary George Canning was also afraid of an effort by the Holy Alliance to reconquer Latin America. Latin America was another new market for British industry that Canning desired to keep open. If Spain or the European powers reconquered Latin America, the mercantilist restrictions would go back into effect. The British were also deeply upset over this French army marching into Spain and this obvious revival of French power in the Old World or in the New World, so Canning called in the U.S. minister, Richard Rush, and suggested a joint Anglo-American note warning the European powers against any intervention in the New World.

President Monroe, when he heard of this, asked Jefferson and Madison for their opinions. Both reacted very favorably and very strongly. Jefferson commented as follows:

> The question presented … is the most momentous which has ever been offered to my contemplation since that of Independence. … Great Britain is the nation which can do us the most harm of any one, or all on earth; and with her on our side we need not fear the whole world.

Take the offer. Monroe's cabinet agreed: Take the offer. Everyone was in favor, except Adams, and Adams convinced the cabinet and Monroe to avoid the bilateral statement and instead issue a unilateral statement. Why?

Adams had already verbalized what would become known as the "non-colonization principle" in the Monroe Doctrine in response to Russian claims in Oregon. He had done so unilaterally in July of 1823. Indeed, he had done so as early as 1821 in a discussion with the British minister to the United States, in which he asserted: "Keep what is yours [in North America], but leave the rest of the continent to us." Now, as a realist, Adams did not think France would invade Latin America to help the Spanish, and he realized that if the French tried, the British fleet would stop the French in their own interest, no matter what the United States did. Furthermore, as an expansionist, Adams did not want his hands tied. Canning's proposal for a bilateral statement contained a clause that neither power desired new territory; Adams clearly did. Furthermore, he didn't want Britain to get the credit in Latin America for any effort to stop the Holy Alliance, and he realized that in any coalition between the still-young and weak United States and the all-powerful British Empire, everyone would say, "Ah-ha, it is the British who are responsible for this." Indeed, as a nationalist, he didn't want such an appearance. As he put it, he didn't want to appear to be "a Yankee cockboat in the wake of a British man-of-war."

He convinced the cabinet and the president to issue a unilateral statement instead of the bilateral statement. So why, then, is it called the Monroe Doctrine instead of the Adams Doctrine? It was President Monroe who insisted on making this statement public. Adams wished to limit it to the diplomatic correspondence. Monroe said, "No, I want the whole world to hear this." It thus appeared in Monroe's annual message to Congress in late 1823, and it bears his name.

What are the major principles? As I previously stated, [the first was] non-colonization: The Western Hemisphere was no longer to be considered open to colonization by the Europeans. In Monroe's words: "The American continents, by the free and independent condition which they have assumed and maintain, are henceforth not to be considered as subjects for future colonization by any European powers." Second [was] "Hands Off" (Non-intervention, Doctrine of the Two Spheres): The two hemispheres constitute not only two distinct geographic areas, but two distinct political areas, one ruled by monarchies and the other consisting of liberty-loving republics. The United States will oppose any effort to extend the European monarchial system to the New World. Again, in Monroe's words: "[W]e should consider any attempt on their part to extend their system to any portion of this hemisphere as dangerous to our peace and safety." Third, in return, the United States would not involve itself in the wars of Europe.

Finally, a principle normally associated with the doctrine, though not directly asserted within it, [was that of] no transfer. This is actually a corollary that was stated separately both before and after the enunciation of the doctrine, though it's implicit within the doctrine. The United States would oppose the transfer of any existing colony in the Western Hemisphere from one European power to another— e.g., France obtaining Cuba as a reward for reconquering Spain's Latin American Empire.

Contrary to popular myth, this doctrine had no legal status whatsoever—not in international law, not in national law; it's simply a presidential statement. It is ignored by the Europeans, at least publicly. Privately, they refer to it as "blustering," "monstrous," "arrogant," and "haughty," but there are no protests. The reason is perhaps best summed up by the Russians, who informed their minister that the doctrine "enunciates views and pretensions so exaggerated, it establishes principles so contrary to the rights of the European powers, that it merits only the most profound contempt"— i.e., silence was the appropriate response. Nor did it prevent European intervention.

What did prevent European intervention in the New World at this time was, as Adams had realized, London's refusal to tolerate such intervention and the power of the British fleet. Indeed, ironically, the issue had already been settled when the cabinet debated the British offer. The offer no longer existed. Canning had decided in October [that] he could not wait for an American response; had met with the French ambassador, [Auguste-Jules-Armand-Marie de] Polignac; and the result had been the so-called Polignac Memorandum, in which Canning made clear British opposition to any French effort to help the Spanish in Latin America, and Polignac had disclaimed any attempt or desire to act in Latin America.

For many decades, British policy and the British fleet would, in effect, enforce the Monroe Doctrine. Canning was at first very pleased with the Monroe Doctrine, stating that he had "called the New World into being to redress the balance of the Old." But he then became angry regarding the non-colonization principle and the competition with the United States for the trade of Latin America. Also, the Anglo-American entente was coming to an end, because while Britain had finally accepted American principles of free trade, as she realized that free trade was in her interest as an industrialized power (the more market she could have open, the better), at the same time, the United States, with its infant industries, was beginning to pass high tariffs against the British to keep British goods out, to protect itself against British competition. What you had in chess might be described here as an *en passant*, as the two sides passed each other. At the moment they passed, you had had the entente, and now they were moving further and further away.

Canning would respond to the Monroe Doctrine by eventually publishing the Polignac Memorandum to make clear to the Latin Americans who was protecting them. He would also recognize the republics of Latin America. Eventually, he would close the West Indies to American shipping when Adams demanded a complete opening and in retaliation for the American high tariffs. Nor were the Latin Americans all that pleased or impressed. The Colombians asked Adams just what the United States intended to do to defend the republics of Latin America. Adams's answer was, at best, extremely vague. By the 1850s, Latin America would see the Monroe Doctrine as merely a cover for U.S. imperialism, no better than the imperialism of the European powers, and it would look primarily to Britain, not the United States.

What, then, had John Quincy Adams and James Monroe actually accomplished? In effect, they boldly reasserted a series of principles that declared the entire hemisphere to be an American sphere of influence, principles that they did not yet have the power to enforce but that Adams realized the British would enforce in their own interests. In doing so, Adams and Monroe had, in effect, fulfilled Washington's prophecy in the Farewell Address: that given time and peace, the United States would be able to bid defiance to the powers of Europe.

Is this Monroe Doctrine a defensive doctrine or an aggressive one? There is historical disagreement on this down to this very day. My answer is yes—it is both defensive and aggressive. It is defensive at the time but aggressive for the future, a future that will be realized in the ensuing decades and with corollaries to the doctrine that we will be exploring in later lectures.

Ironically, however, Adams would soon turn against the aggressive expansionism that he had done so much to promote as secretary of state, specifically in regard to the Mexican War and the expansion of slavery. Yet even earlier, Adams had warned Americans against militant aggression and against going abroad on ideological crusades to remake the world, warnings that were clearly prescient. Adams toned down what had been, in the Monroe Doctrine, Monroe's very strong denunciations of French intervention in Spain and praise for the Greek revolution against the Turks. Adams toned all of these down to simply good wishes.

Even earlier, in response to an 1821 claim by Henry Clay that the United States should immediately recognize all the republics of Latin America because the United States had a mission to promote liberty around the world—in response to that, Adams, on July 4, 1821, stated the following (America, according to Adams):

> Wherever the standard of freedom and independence has been or shall be unfurled, there will her heart, her benedictions and her prayers be, but she goes not abroad in search of monsters to destroy. She is the well-wisher to the freedom and independence of all. She is the champion and vindicator only of her own. She will commend the general cause by the countenance of her voice and the benign sympathy of her example. She well knows that by once enlisting under other banners than her own, were they even the banners of foreign independence, she would involve herself beyond the power of extrication, in all the wars of interest and intrigue, of individual avarice, envy, and ambition, which assume the colors and usurp the standard of freedom. The fundamental maxims of her policy would insensibly change from *liberty* to *force*. ... She might become the dictatress of the world. She would be no longer the ruler of her own spirit.

Within this quote and with his policies, John Quincy Adams boldly reasserted the realist tradition in U.S. foreign policy. It is a tradition many of his successors would heed and many of his successors would not heed. The extent to which it should be heeded constitutes, to this very day, a major debate in U.S. foreign policy.

Lecture Eight
"Manifest Destiny" and War with Mexico

Scope:

The diplomacy of John Quincy Adams ushered in a period of enormous territorial expansion across the North American continent that, by 1848, included the acquisition of Oregon, Texas, California, and New Mexico—the first by treaty but the others by war. This period also witnessed the expulsion of the Native American tribes east of the Mississippi River. Americans justified their expansionist behavior by an ideology known as "Manifest Destiny." This lecture explains that ideology and examines the specific territorial acquisitions of the 1840s, with a particular emphasis on the role of President James K. Polk.

Outline

I. The 1830s and 1840s would witness an enormous burst of territorial expansion.

    A. Americans defined and justified this expansion as Manifest Destiny—a term coined by New York newspaper editor John O'Sullivan in 1839.

        1. The United States, according to O'Sullivan, was a special nation destined by God's will to expand over the entire continent and, perhaps, the entire hemisphere and to become the greatest nation in world history.

        2. O'Sullivan saw this as a peaceful process of settlers moving westward, but the reality would be quite aggressive and would involve numerous military conflicts, including a war with Mexico.

    B. This aggressive expansionism was partially the result of changes in American thought patterns.

        1. This was the age of the "common man" in politics and *laissez-faire* capitalism in economics.

        2. These thought patterns reinforced the old Jeffersonian link between democracy and landed expansion by emphasizing the frontier as the place where individualism and upward social mobility could flourish, with President Andrew Jackson (1767–1845) himself as the great symbol of this frontier democracy.

3. Native American tribalism stood as the antithesis to this value system of individualism and material acquisitiveness.

4. The religious revival known as the Second Great Awakening, with its democratization of salvation and perfectionist doctrines, also played a role in this expansion by reinforcing the belief that the United States was God's chosen nation.

5. Simultaneously, a new "scientific" racism developed in both Europe and the United States that allowed Americans to argue that they were genetically, politically, and culturally superior and, therefore, had the right to dispossess "inferior" peoples who inhabited the land they desired.

6. Furthermore, the Enlightenment values and internationalism of the nation's Founding Fathers disappeared with their passing, to be replaced by the intense provincialism and nationalism of their children.

C. Expansionism was also the result of the development of steamboats and railroads, a transportation revolution that made possible growth across the continent.

D. Sectional interests of the West, the South, and the North played a role in continental expansionism, as well.

E. Paradoxically, this super-confident nationalism coexisted with a paranoid fear of threats from abroad. Europeans, Americans feared, were plotting to thwart American expansion in order to expand themselves, thereby justifying American growth as a defensive move.

II. The clear precursors to this major burst of landed expansion were the actions of John Quincy Adams and the removal of the eastern Native American tribes to the area west of the Mississippi River in the 1820s and 1830s.

A. The War of 1812 had been a disaster for these tribes and had broken their power to resist American encroachment.

B. Between 1826 and 1840, the United States would sign approximately 100 treaties with Native American tribes involving acquisition of their lands.

C. The most famous—or infamous—case was the removal of the Cherokees from Georgia and Tennessee against their will in the 1830s, accomplished under the terms of the 1830 Indian Removal Act signed by President Jackson.

III. While Native American tribes were being removed to land west of the Mississippi River, American settlers were flocking to the northern Mexican province of Texas.

    A. The Spanish and Mexican governments had first encouraged such settlement as a means of creating a buffer state to block U.S. government efforts to annex it, but that policy boomeranged by creating a Trojan Horse with 30,000 loyal Americans in Texas.

    B. When the dictator Santa Anna seized power in Mexico and attempted to centralize, these settlers successfully revolted, declared a republic, and requested annexation to the United States as a slave state.

    C. Presidents Jackson and Van Buren both rejected annexation because of fears that it would exacerbate the slavery issue at home and lead to war with Mexico. Texas was, thus, left to defend itself against a Mexico that constantly threatened reconquest.

    D. Texans were supported by the British, who desired an independent entity to block further U.S. expansion. British support, in turn, led many Americans to favor annexation as a way to block the British!

    E. In 1843–1844, President John Tyler pressed for annexation, but the Senate refused to agree.

    F. In the presidential election of 1844, the Democratic winner, James K. Polk (1795–1849), strongly supported annexation. The now lame-duck Tyler resubmitted an annexation measure. The Senate barely agreed, with a vote of 27 to 25, whereupon Tyler signed the measure, three days before Polk was inaugurated. The new president thus inherited a diplomatic crisis with Mexico.

    G. Tension with Britain during the 1830s and 1840s also involved disagreements over the Canadian-American boundary; Maine, Minnesota, and the Pacific Northwest; and American support for the Canadian Rebellion of 1837.

IV. Polk, the new president, was a rabid expansionist who would use the Texas issue to initiate a war with Mexico for the acquisition of California and simultaneously threaten war with England over Oregon.

    A. During the presidential campaign of 1844, Polk had combined the Texas and Oregon issues by calling for the "re-annexation" of Texas and "reoccupation" of the entire Oregon Territory. He did so as a means of overcoming the sectional divide over slavery and forming a national consensus in favor of expansion.

    B. After a year of both diplomacy and threats of war, Polk agreed to a compromise with Britain that divided the Oregon Territory at the 49th degree north latitude—though he insisted that the Senate first advise him to accept this compromise.

    C. Simultaneously, he used a combination of diplomacy and threats of war over the boundary of Texas to force Mexico to sell California. In this case, war ensued, with Polk using his presidential powers as commander in chief to force a military confrontation, then manipulating the subsequent vote in Congress so that opponents could not dissent without appearing unpatriotic.

        1. To minimize those divisions and associated political problems, Polk planned a short and limited war in which U.S. forces would quickly secure the disputed Texas border and seize California and New Mexico. They rapidly did so, but Mexico refused to surrender.

        2. Consequently, Polk sent additional military forces under General Winfield Scott to invade central Mexico.

        3. Scott's conquest of Mexico City led many Americans—including Polk—to consider annexation of the entire country.

        4. But when a new Mexican government finally agreed to Polk's original territorial terms, he accepted the treaty as the best means of ending what had become a highly unpopular and divisive war.

V. Historians disagree sharply in their assessment of Polk and this era of expansion. Many admire him for his territorial acquisitions, while others condemn him for initiating a war of aggression that had devastating long-term consequences.

Suggested Readings:

Horsman, *Race and Manifest Destiny.*

Pletcher, *The Diplomacy of Annexation.*

Stephanson, *Manifest Destiny.*

Weeks, *Building the Continental Empire.*

Questions to Consider:

1. What were the most important factors in the burst of American continental expansion that occurred in the years between the end of the War of 1812 and 1848?

2. Does James K. Polk deserve the reputation as a near-great president that he has received in several presidential polls? Why?

Lecture Eight—Transcript
"Manifest Destiny" and War with Mexico

The 1830s and 1840s would witness an enormous burst of American territorial expansion. This expansion was defined and justified by a term: "Manifest Destiny." It was a term coined by the New York newspaper editor John O'Sullivan in 1839. The United States, according to O'Sullivan, was a special nation—God's chosen, destined by God's will to expand over the entire North American continent and, perhaps, over the entire hemisphere and to become the greatest nation in world history. Its democracy was to be the earthly equivalent of Christianity, and its cause thus equal both to humanity's cause and to God's cause.

The entire process was supposed to be peaceful—settlers moving westward, taking over an area, Americanizing it, and becoming part of the Union. But the reality during the 1830s and 1840s was quite aggressive and involved numerous military conflicts, including a full-scale war with Mexico. This highly aggressive expansionism was partially the result of major changes in American thought patterns in the early 19th century. This was the era of Jacksonian democracy, the era of "rugged individualism" and the "common man." Property qualifications for voting ceased. All white males were able to vote. Government run by educated elites ceased to be the norm; instead, what you had was the rise of professional politicians and political parties as we know them today. Anything considered elitist was attacked. Simultaneously, you had the rise of *laissez-faire* capitalism—get the government out of controlling the economy in any way and allow individual free enterprise to run uncontrolled. Adam Smith's "hidden hand" would work.

The link between this political democracy and this economic belief system was clearly seen in the so-called Bank War. Andrew Jackson, as president, vetoed the recharter bill for the second National Bank of the United States and removed government funds from the National Bank. Jackson attacked the National Bank as an unfair collusion between government and a single elitist corporation that had special government privileges. Jackson, interestingly enough, was supported not only by "common" men but also by the new Wall Street bankers in New York, desirous of overthrowing the power and control exercised by the National Bank on Chestnut Street in Philadelphia. It was an immensely popular move, but it would result in financial chaos and the panic/depression of 1837. This link between the political and the economic could also be seen in the rise of professional politicians during this time and the spoils system. Politics itself became a business in this country.

What in the world does all of this have to do with landed expansion? These political and economic ideologies further cemented the old Jeffersonian link between democracy and landed expansion by emphasizing the frontier as the place for upward socioeconomic mobility and where individualism could flourish. Jackson himself was a westerner; he was the symbol of all of this. Furthermore, the antithesis of this entire value system of individualism, of material acquisitiveness, is Indian tribalism, and it is far from accidental in this regard that Indians are dispossessed of their land during this time period.

The entire movement is also reinforced by a major religious revival during this time, the so-called Second Great Awakening. Salvation was now available to all through the conversion experience. Anybody could be saved, but if you were saved, it was then your responsibility to help perfect the world. There was a strong belief that perfection of the world could be done and that it would hasten the Second Coming. All of this reinforced the belief that the United States was God's chosen instrument because this perfection was to take place here. If you put this whole thing together, what you get is that what is good for the United States is good for the world and is part of God's will.

At the same time in Europe and the United States, you get the rise of a new "scientific" racism linked to new scientific discoveries and the replacement of Enlightenment ideals of universalism with the Romantic era's emphasis on particularity. The belief grows that Anglo-Saxons are genetically superior, as well as culturally and religiously superior to others. Racism is not new during the 1830s and '40s, but this justification is, and with it comes the belief that Anglo-Saxons have the right to dispossess the "inferior" people who inhabit the land. You had an entire science based around this—phrenology, the measurement of skull sizes and shapes to prove the superiority of certain racial groups.

Furthermore, the Enlightenment values and internationalism of the Founding Fathers were now gone. A new generation has arisen, one that was incredibly provincial, as well as incredibly nationalistic.

Furthermore, as noted in the last lecture, the new transportation technology of steamboats and railroads meant that expansion across the entire continent was now possible. The old problem that Jefferson had faced—how [to] have representative government if it will take the representative from Oregon his entire term of office simply to travel to Washington and back home—is now gone. Now you have the technical ability to link an entire continent together.

There are also concrete sectional interests involved in the expansion that takes place during the 1830s and the 1840s. Western settlers want new land for settlement. Southerners want new land for their cotton culture. Cotton depletes the soil, so new land is constantly needed. They also want more land so as to maintain a sectional balance between slave states and free states in the U.S. Senate. Similarly, northerners want more land in order to obtain more free states, but in addition, northeasterners in particular want ports on the Pacific Coast for the burgeoning trade that is taking place with islands in the Pacific and Asia.

In this regard, it is important to keep in mind that landed expansion coincided with trade expansion in the Pacific and Asia and with missionary activity in the Pacific and Asia stemming from the Second Great Awakening. This is especially the case in Hawaii and in China. Indeed, the first U.S. treaty with China, the Treaty of Wangxia, is signed in 1844 in the midst of this era. The United States will also develop a major interest in the Hawaiian Islands as a way station, as well as a whaling station and another opportunity for American missionaries. By the 1840s, merchants, whalers, and missionaries had established a major U.S. influence in the Hawaiian Islands. Indeed, in the so-called Tyler Doctrine of 1842 (named after President John Tyler), the United States, in effect, extended the Monroe Doctrine to Hawaii by warning other powers to stay away.

A decade later, in 1853–1854, a naval force under Commodore Matthew Perry would open the previously isolated kingdom of Japan via the Treaty of Kanagawa. Much of this was the work of Daniel Webster, secretary of state during two different presidencies and senator from Massachusetts, and his idea of a great commercial chain extending across the Pacific to Asia.

This entire super-confident nationalism paradoxically coexisted with a paranoid fear of threats from Europe, especially from Great Britain, which was supposedly plotting to thwart U.S. expansion in order to expand itself. In American minds, this plot by the British justified American expansion as a defensive move against the British. Keep that in mind as we proceed in this lecture.

The clear precursors to this burst of territorial expansion were the moves of John Quincy Adams, discussed in the last lecture, and the removal of the eastern Indian tribes to the area west of the Mississippi River during the 1820s and the 1830s. The War of 1812 had been a disaster for these tribes. Tecumseh's confederation had been smashed, Northwest and Southwest. Indeed, Indian power to resist white encroachment had been broken. Between 1826 and 1840, the United States would sign approximately 100 treaties with Indian tribes involving acquisition of their lands and movement of the tribes west of the Mississippi.

The most famous—or infamous—such case is the removal of the Cherokee Indians from Georgia and Tennessee against their will in the 1830s. This was done under the terms of the 1830 Indian Removal Act that President Andrew Jackson had requested and received from Congress. That act allowed him to set aside land in the West and exchange it for Indian lands east of the Mississippi. The Cherokees, who had adopted an American form of government, an American culture, resisted Jackson. They also resisted the efforts of the state of Georgia to extend its laws to them. Their case went all the way to the United States Supreme Court, where Chief Justice John Marshall labeled the Indian tribes a "domestic dependent nation" and, thus, under federal control, not state control (i.e., Georgia could not extend its laws to the Cherokees). President Jackson supposedly commented: "Chief Justice Marshall has made his decision; let him enforce it." Jackson did nothing to enforce it but, indeed, encouraged Georgia to resist the court and helped in the dispossession and forced removal of the Cherokee Indians along the notorious Trail of Tears.

At the same time that this is happening, American settlers are flocking to Texas, which is part of, at first, the Spanish Empire and, then, an independent Mexico. These Americans had been encouraged by the Spaniards and then by the Mexican government in order to help create a buffer state in this very sparsely settled area to block future U.S. expansion. But the policy boomeranged. In effect, what was created here was a Trojan Horse of 30,000 Americans in Texas who retained their loyalty to the United States and who violated

Spanish and Mexican insistence that they convert to Roman Catholicism and not practice slavery.

When the Mexican dictator Santa Anna seized power and attempted to centralize, these Texans revolted against his rule in 1835–1836. They declared the Republic of Texas. After initial military defeats, they, in turn, defeated Santa Anna at the Battle of San Jacinto, and they request annexation to the United States. President Jackson and his successor, President Martin Van Buren, said no. The reason: fear of the slavery issue at home ripping the nation apart over admission of Texas and fear of a war with Mexico. Texas was, thus, left as an independent entity to defend itself against a Mexico that consistently threatened reconquest.

Texan independence was supported by the British in an effort to block further U.S. expansion, but that British support, in turn, led many Americans to favor annexation as a way to block the British. In 1843–1844, President Tyler thus pushed for annexation, but the Senate refused to agree. Then, in the 1844 presidential election, the Democratic winner, James K. Polk of Tennessee, strongly supports annexation. His victory had been quite narrow, but he interpreted that victory as a mandate for expansion; so did John Tyler, the lame-duck president. Polk would not take office until March. Seeing it as a mandate for expansion and fearing what the British were trying to do, Tyler resubmitted the annexation measure. But instead of submitting it as a treaty that would require a two-thirds vote in the Senate, he submitted it as a joint resolution that only required a majority vote in each house of Congress. The Senate agreed by the barest of votes, 27 to 25. Tyler signed the bill three days before the inauguration of James K. Polk as president. Mexico broke diplomatic relations, and Polk, as he is inaugurated president, thus inherits a diplomatic crisis with Mexico.

Trouble was also brewing simultaneously with the British in the 1830s and early 1840s over the boundary in the Northeast, in Maine and all the way to Minnesota. You had, along the Maine-New Brunswick boundary, a minor war of sorts, known as the Aroostook War. You had had American support for Canadian rebels, who were trying to declare independence from Great Britain in 1837, and you had conflict in Oregon, especially after 1841, when "Oregon fever" began—a boom in settlement touched off by Protestant missionaries in the Willamette Valley reporting on the lush conditions and land available there. The number of American settlers jumped from 700 to 5,000.

In 1841 and 1842, Secretary of State Daniel Webster signed a treaty with Lord Ashburton of Britain that resolved many of these issues but not the Oregon issue. The old disagreement discussed in the last lecture over where to divide the Oregon Territory remained, with Britain pressing for the Columbia River and the United States pressing for Puget Sound.

The new president, James K. Polk, a rabid expansionist, would use the Texas boundary issue—not the annexation of Texas but the Texas boundary issue—to initiate a war with Mexico in order to obtain California from Mexico. Simultaneously, he would threaten war with England over the Oregon boundary.

During the presidential campaign of 1844, Polk had combined the Texas and Oregon issues. His platform had called for the "re-annexation" of Texas and the "reoccupation" of the entire Oregon Territory up to the boundary with Alaska, 54 degrees, 40 minutes [54°40']; "54/40 or Fight" became the battle cry. The logic here was that John Quincy Adams had incorrectly given up Texas, and Oregon had, similarly, belonged to the United States and the Whigs had given it up. Polk was, of course, a Democrat. But what he is actually doing is trying to overcome the sectional divide over slavery and form a national consensus in favor of expansion by offering the South something and the North something. Polk also wants California for Mexico and fears that the British are going to try to take it first.

In 1845, Polk will reassert the Monroe Doctrine against the British over both Oregon and California. After a year of both diplomacy and threats of war, Polk agreed to a compromise with Britain that divided the Oregon Territory at the 49th degree north latitude, thereby giving the United States the portion of Puget Sound that it had wanted. But he submitted this treaty first to the Senate for previous advice on whether or not to accept this compromise. The Senate, according to the Constitution, is supposed to advise and consent on treaties. Presidents traditionally have only asked the Senate to consent. In this case, Polk asked the Senate to advise before he even signed the treaty. That way, if the Senate said, "Sign it," Polk could claim to his rabid supporters, who might attack him for giving up on 54/40, "The Senate told me to do it. It advised me to do it." The Senate then voted 38 to 12 that Polk sign the treaty. He signed it on June 15, resubmitted it for ratification, and the Senate ratified the treaty on June 18 by a vote of 41 to 14.

A second reason why Polk agreed to this compromise was that by June, war had already begun with Mexico. Polk had used a combination of diplomacy and threats of war over the appropriate boundary of Texas as a means of forcing Mexico to sell California to the United States. He sent a peace mission under John Slidell to Mexico City in an attempt to purchase California, but simultaneously, he sent General Zachary Taylor and the U.S. Army into the disputed territory between the Nueces River and the Rio Grande River, in case the Mexicans would not agree to a peaceful settlement. They did not, and in this case, war ensued.

Mexico rejected Slidell, and Polk decided on war, even before he found out that Mexican and American troops had clashed in the disputed territory. That became a convenient excuse, and on May 11th, Polk requested war on the grounds that American blood had been shed upon American soil. But the actual congressional declaration of war was attached as a "rider" to a military appropriations bill. This was a political ploy that made it nearly impossible for opponents to object. American troops are under attack; are you going to oppose the military appropriations that those troops need? In addition, the Whig opposition had bitter memories of what had happened to the Federalist Party when it objected to the War of 1812 at the Hartford Convention. So the Congress votes overwhelmingly for war, but this overwhelming vote masks serious dissent within the Congress.

What we also see here is an enormous expansion of presidential war-making power. Using his authority as the commander in chief, Polk had placed an army in harm's way in disputed territory and, thereby, obtained the war that he wanted.

The war that Polk had planned was a limited one in which U.S. forces would quickly secure the disputed Texan border and seize California and New Mexico. They quickly did so, aided by a revolt of American settlers in California led by the American consul in Monterey, Thomas Larkin, and "The Pathfinder," John C. Frémont, who was exploring with the Army Corps of Topographical Engineers in California at that time. The interesting question was why he was in Mexican territory at that point. But even after the acquisition of the

Texan border, New Mexico, and California, Mexico refused to surrender. Consequently, Polk sent additional military forces under General Winfield Scott to invade central Mexico. Scott took Veracruz, marched inland, and conquered Mexico City. He had taken the whole country.

This led many Americans, including Polk, to consider annexing all of Mexico, not just the northern territories. But when Polk's emissary, the chief clerk of the State Department, Nicholas P. Trist, ignored a presidential recall order and negotiated a peace treaty (the Treaty of Guadalupe Hidalgo) with a new Mexican government that was willing to agree to Polk's original territorial terms, Polk accepted the ensuing treaty. To him, it was the best means of ending what had become, by this point, a highly unpopular and divisive war that was wrecking his party and dramatically increasing sectional tensions.

It is our own president who began this war, said Representative Garrett Davis of Kentucky. He has been carrying it out for months in a series of acts. Congress, which is vested exclusively by the Constitution with war-making power, he has not deigned to consult. Much less to ask it for any authority. Another congressman from Illinois defied Polk to show the spot on which American blood had been shed upon American soil. He became known by the nickname "Spot" or "Spotty"; his other name, by which we know him, was Abraham Lincoln. He was not reelected to Congress.

In the Senate, [there was] similar dissent. Senator Daniel Webster said that he concurred with a House resolution claiming that: "the war with Mexico was begun unconstitutionally and unnecessarily by the Executive Government of the United States." It had been done to obtain territory for new slave states, which would disrupt the sectional balance. "I think I see," said Webster, "a course adopted that is likely to turn the Constitution under which we live into a deformed monster" based on inequality and, perhaps, lead to the breakup of the Union.

By the terms of the Treaty of Guadalupe Hidalgo, Texas would be annexed to the United States, with the Rio Grande as the boundary. California and New Mexico would also become part of the United States. In return, the United States would pay the Mexican government $15 million and assume $3.25 million in claims that

American citizens held against the Mexican government. The Senate would concur by a vote of 38 to 14.

Historians disagree very sharply in their assessment of James K. Polk and this era of continental expansion. Many historians consider the relatively unknown Polk to be a near-great president. The reason? These enormous territorial acquisitions of Oregon, California, New Mexico, and the Texan boundary were acquisitions that made the United States a continental power, stretching from the Atlantic to the Pacific Ocean. But other historians condemn him; they argue that he initiated a war of aggression against Mexico, one that had devastating long-term consequences. What were they? They were the permanent enmity of the peoples of Latin America [and] dangerously expanded presidential war-making powers. It is Polk who first shows those war-making powers—what the president, as commander in chief, can do to manipulate a war that he wants. But most immediately, there is dramatically increased sectional conflict at home, as Americans now argue bitterly over whether to allow slavery to expand into the newly acquired territories.

In August of 1846, David Wilmot of Pennsylvania introduces a proviso known, of course, as the Wilmot Proviso, to ban slavery in any territory acquired as a result of the war with Mexico. That led to furious debate that would tie up Congress for the next four years. The ensuing sectional conflict of the 1850s and 1860s would block almost all future expansionist efforts and would eventually lead to civil war. There are numerous expansionist efforts—as we will see—during the 1850s, but with one exception, they will all fail. The major reason they will fail is the issue of expansion of slavery. Similarly, the issue of expansion of slavery is the issue that will lead to civil war—not slavery itself but the question of expansion of slavery into the territories of the United States acquired by this war, as well as previously acquired. That civil war is, of course, going to threaten American power in the world, but beyond that, it is going to threaten the very continued existence of the nation.

In the next lecture, we will look at the failed expansionist efforts of the 1850s and follow that with a look at the diplomacy of the Civil War and the reasons the Union was able to prevail. That, in turn, will set the stage for the rise of the United States to superpower status in the late 19th and early 20th centuries.

Lecture Nine
Causes and Diplomacy of the Civil War

Scope:

The territorial acquisitions of the 1840s enormously exacerbated sectional tensions and played a major role in the outbreak of Civil War in 1861. This lecture will first explore the relationship between territorial expansion and the coming of the Civil War, then focus on Union and Confederate diplomacy during that conflict. British and French intervention on the side of the South was a distinct possibility, and it would have virtually guaranteed Confederate victory in the same way that French intervention in the War for Independence led to American victory over the British. Such intervention appeared quite likely, especially in 1861–1862, but it never materialized. This lecture seeks to explain why through an examination of both southern and northern diplomacy with the European powers.

Outline

I. The conquest and acquisition of Texas, California, and New Mexico led to massive debate over whether slavery should be extended into new territories and doomed additional efforts at expansion during the 1850s.

A. The debate over the Wilmot Proviso banning slavery in territories acquired from Mexico tied up Congress until 1850, when a major compromise was finally reached.

B. Because that compromise admitted California into the union as a free state, southerners searched desperately for more conquests in Central America and the Caribbean—most notably, in Cuba—to reestablish sectional balance in the Senate.

C. The California Gold Rush of 1849 reinforced expansionist efforts in Central America, particularly in Nicaragua and Panama, in order to construct a canal or railroad for easy and quick transit to California.

D. These expansionist efforts were supported by President Franklin Pierce (1804–1869), who actively sought to obtain Cuba from Spain, and by independent soldiers of fortune, known as filibusters, who attempted to create private empires in Central America and the Caribbean. But most such efforts failed militarily and politically.

E. Southerners also pressed for and obtained, with the Kansas-Nebraska Act of 1854, an overthrow of the 1820 Missouri Compromise ban on slavery north of the 36°30' parallel in the Louisiana Purchase. This led to virtual civil war in Kansas and the creation of the sectional Republican Party, which opposed any slavery expansion into the territories. The party's electoral successes by 1860 led directly to southern secession and civil war.

II. Confederate diplomacy during the Civil War focused on obtaining British and French recognition and aid. If successful, such recognition and aid would be as important in ensuring Confederate independence as French recognition and aid had been in ensuring American independence during the Revolutionary War.

A. Britain and France had numerous reasons to support the South.

1. A permanently divided United States would pose less of a threat to their possessions and interests in the Western Hemisphere.

2. Napoleon III of France was determined to conquer Mexico, and the success of this mission required negation of any effective U.S. opposition.

3. The critical British textile industry relied on the South's cotton.

B. Knowing the importance of cotton, the South placed an embargo on its sale as a means of forcing British intervention.

C. France would not act without Britain, and numerous factors also argued against British recognition and intervention.

1. Britain had a huge surplus of cotton and cotton goods in 1861.

2. Britain also relied on the North's foodstuffs.

3. Britain opposed and had already abolished slavery within its empire.

4. As an empire, Britain was loath to support rebellion.

5. Union Secretary of State William Henry Seward (1801–1872) threatened war if Britain recognized or aided the Confederacy.

6. European diplomatic tradition dictated that a government should not be recognized until it had shown its ability to maintain independence.

    D. Given all these factors, British behavior would depend to a great extent on military and political events during the war.

III. In retrospect, the strongest possibility of European intervention came in 1861–1862.

    A. In 1861, a crisis occurred over Union seizure of Confederate diplomats from the British mail ship *Trent*, but President Lincoln (1809–1865) and Seward backed down under British pressure and the crisis ended.

    B. In the summer and early fall of 1862, Confederate military victories led the British to seriously consider a mediation offer that would have led to recognition.

    C. A divided British government decided to await the outcome of General Lee's first invasion of the North, which ended with a tactical draw at the battle of Antietam. Antietam put an end to Lee's invasion, provided Lincoln with the opportunity to issue the Emancipation Proclamation, and caused the British government to decide against mediation.

    D. Never again would the British come so close to intervening, and major Union military victories in 1863–1864 ended any realistic possibility of such intervention.

    E. Additional crises erupted in 1863 over the building of British commerce raiders and warships for the Confederacy, but a diplomatic rupture was avoided through astute diplomacy on both sides, and the issues were finally resolved in the 1871 Treaty of Washington.

    F. The failure to obtain British recognition and intervention was a major factor in the Confederate loss, a defeat that guaranteed continued American dominance in the Western Hemisphere and growing status as a great power.

    G. The Confederate defeat also marked the triumph of the industrial North over the agrarian South, thereby guaranteeing both continued industrial expansion and a more centralized and powerful national government. These would be vital components in the emergence of the United States as a great power.

IV. Seward illustrated the nation's emerging great-power status immediately after the war when he moved to force the French out of Mexico.

    A. During the Civil War, Napoleon III had succeeded in conquering Mexico and installing the Austrian Archduke Maximilian as emperor.

    B. Seward made clear his opposition to this violation of the Monroe Doctrine but was powerless to act during the Civil War.

    C. In 1865, Seward increased his diplomatic protests to Paris and sent substantial troops to the Mexican border. In early 1866, he demanded and obtained a French military withdrawal and blocked any Austrian intervention.

    D. Although some historians credit this result and Maximilian's subsequent demise to Mexican guerrilla warfare and European preoccupations, others have argued that Seward's pressure forced both the French and the Austrians to back down, successfully illustrating that the United States had already attained great-power status.

Suggested Readings:

Crook, *The North, the South, and the Powers, 1861–1865.*

Jones, *Union in Peril.*

May, *The Southern Dream of a Caribbean Empire, 1854–1861.*

Owsley, *King Cotton Diplomacy.*

Questions to Consider:

1. Compare and contrast the factors that led France to intervene in the American War for Independence with the factors that led Great Britain and France not to intervene in the American Civil War. How do you account for the Confederate failure to repeat the earlier American success in obtaining European intervention?

2. In what ways did Union victory in the Civil War virtually guarantee great-power status for the United States?

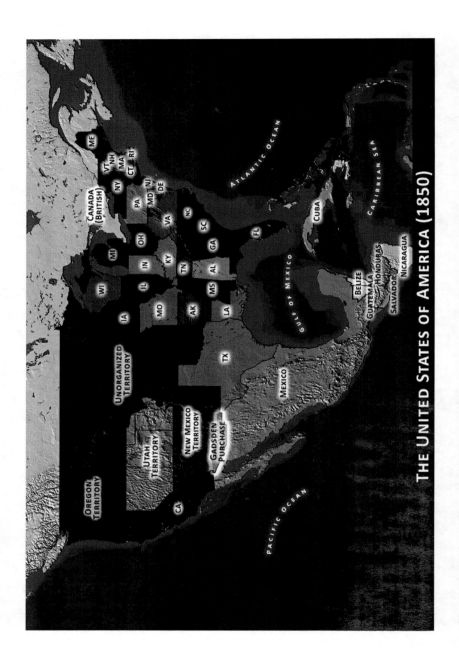

THE UNITED STATES OF AMERICA (1850)

©2008 The Teaching Company.

Lecture Nine—Transcript
Causes and Diplomacy of the Civil War

The acquisition of Mexican territory between 1846 and 1848 led to a massive debate in Congress and the public at large over the extension of slavery into these new territories. That debate would doom most additional efforts at territorial expansion in the 1850s.

As noted in the last lecture, the Wilmot Proviso banning slavery in the territories acquired from the war with Mexico tied up Congress for four years. In 1850, a major compromise was finally reached—known as, of course, the Compromise of 1850. California was admitted as a free state, and the slave trade was abolished in Washington, DC. Those were two components favorable to the North. In return, the issue of slavery in the rest of the Mexican cession—basically, present-day New Mexico, Arizona, and portions of other states—would be decided by the principle of popular sovereignty. The actual settlers living there would decide whether or not to have slavery, and a new, tough Fugitive Slave Law was added as part of the compromise package.

Why is California admitted as a state, skipping the territorial stage? The 1849 Gold Rush led to an explosion in the population of California. Thus, California, by 1850, had enough inhabitants to skip the territorial stage and apply directly for statehood as a free state. Because it is so admitted within the Compromise of 1850 and because slavery was barred north of the line 36 degrees, 30 minutes [36°30'] north latitude in the Louisiana Purchase by the Missouri Compromise of 1820, southerners in the 1850s searched desperately for more territory in which [they] could have slavery to create more slave states in order to regain and maintain a sectional balance within the United States Senate. The area in which they look is Central America and the Caribbean, and that is where expansionist efforts shall center in the 1850s.

The California Gold Rush also gives impetus to additional expansionist efforts in Central America in order to construct a canal and/or a railroad for easy and quick transit to California. There is no transcontinental railroad at this time; the quickest way to get to California is to go down to Central America, somehow cross either the Isthmus of Panama or Nicaragua, and then [go] up the coast to California. It beats going around all of South America, and more and more interest is expressed in building a canal. Indeed, a railroad will be built in Nicaragua by Cornelius Vanderbilt. These two areas, Nicaragua and Panama, are of particular interest because they contain the best potential canal routes.

Expansion into Central America and the Caribbean was strongly supported by the pro-southern administration of Franklin Pierce, a Democrat, who is elected in 1852 and takes office in 1853. That expansion is also supported by an extraordinary group of soldiers of fortune (known as filibusters), with Narciso López, John Quitman, and William Walker being three of the most famous. What these individuals try to do is conquer areas and set them up as private empires, and they are supported by southern expansionists. López will try to invade Cuba in 1849, in 1850, and in 1851. He will eventually be captured and executed by the Spanish authorities in Cuba.

The most famous of these filibusters is William Walker, the gray-eyed man of destiny. In 1853, Walker will attempt to conquer Baja, California. In 1855, he will succeed in taking over the government of Nicaragua. He will join one side in a Nicaraguan civil war, and then he will seize the presidency. In 1856, he will be recognized by the Pierce administration in Washington, but he is then overthrown when he attempted to reinstitute slavery and alienated the railroad and shipping magnate Cornelius Vanderbilt, who had very strong interests in Nicaragua. Walker was forced to flee. He tried to return in 1857. He tried again in 1858, and finally, in 1860, he was captured and shot by the Hondurans.

The simultaneous diplomatic efforts by the Pierce administration to acquire territory would focus on Cuba. The acquisition of Cuba was an old American dream, ever since the days of Thomas Jefferson. What you had were these constant—what I refer to as—fruit analogies. Cuba, only 90 miles from the United States, will "fall like a ripe apple," one president would say; "like a ripe plum," another would say; "like a ripe pear," a third would say. So it's an old idea, an old issue, but there is a new aggressiveness in the 1850s, and now the reason is openly to get a new slave state because there is slavery in Cuba. There is also a desire to get Cuba before the Spanish perhaps abolish slavery or before there is a successful slave insurrection, which could lead to a new former-slave republic, like Haiti.

Polk will attempt to purchase Cuba for $100 million in 1848. Compare that to what he was willing to pay for the Texan boundary, California, and New Mexico. He will fail. He will also get transit rights across Panama from Colombia at this time in a treaty that we will return to when we get to the building of the Panama Canal. Panama is a province of Colombia. Keep that in mind.

President Pierce will also try to obtain Cuba. Specifically, he will threaten war in 1854 over an affair known as the "Black Warrior," where an American ship was incorrectly seized by Spanish authorities. Pierce tried to use this to force the Spanish to sell Cuba or to have the United States take it by force. Pierce had his emissaries try to purchase Cuba for up to $130 million. That led to a famous document in the history of American foreign policy, the so-called Ostend Manifesto, written by three American ministers in Europe—Pierre Soulé, John Mason, and James Buchanan—in which they proposed that the United States attempt to purchase Cuba for up to $120 million and, if that failed, to seize it forcibly. Well, the Ostend Manifesto also fails when it becomes public. It led to an explosion within the North and within Congress. Indeed, all such efforts to acquire Cuba or any other territory will fail, blocked primarily by northern opposition to the extension of slavery.

The one exception, the only successful territorial purchase during the 1850s, is the small Gadsden Purchase. In present-day southern New Mexico and Arizona, in 1853, approximately 30,000 square miles are purchased from Mexico for $10 million. Santa Anna is back in power and needs more money. The reason for purchasing this piece of territory is a southern railroad route. There is talk of a transcontinental railroad and whether that route shall be northern or southern. The Gadsden Purchase is needed for the southern route. It's the only successful territorial purchase. The territorial expansion has become a totally sectional issue by this time.

The British will also act to check U.S. attempted expansion in the Caribbean and Central America at this time. They, too, wish to have a canal through Central America, but they wish to create it. They also have extensive interest in Central America and the Caribbean. By 1850, the United States and Britain each fear each other sufficiently to sign a treaty, the Clayton-Bulwer Treaty, saying that neither side would ever monopolize or fortify a canal or attempt to colonize the area. Each one signs it for fear the other is about to do it.

Again, when we get to the building of the Panama Canal in a future lecture, we will talk more about this.

The point for this time period is that continental expansion came to an end in the 1850s; commercial expansion in the Pacific did not. As previously mentioned, Commodore Perry's opening of Japan in the Treaty of Kanagawa will occur in 1853–1854, but it is the sectional issue over expansion of slavery into the territories that dominates American politics at this time.

In 1853–1854, southerners had pressed for and obtained, in the Kansas-Nebraska Act, an overthrow of the 1820 Missouri Compromise ban on slavery north of the line 36/30 in the Louisiana Purchase. Instead, as with the rest of the Mexican cession, you will have popular sovereignty. Let the people living in the area decide. This passed primarily because Stephen Douglas of Illinois found that this was the price that he had to pay for southern support for a bill to organize the Kansas and Nebraska territories, which you had to do in order to have a transcontinental railroad going through those territories and into Chicago in Douglas's home state of Illinois.

Many northerners were furious, and the opening of the Kansas and Nebraska territories to slavery via popular sovereignty led both sides to pour armed volunteers into the Kansas Territory in a virtual civil war. "Bleeding Kansas" would dominate the 1850s and was a clear prelude to what would occur nationally from 1861 to 1865. The act also led to the collapse of the Whig Party under the impact of the slavery issue and the creation of the new Republican Party, a party that opposed any slavery expansion into the territories. Again, please note that it is this issue—the expansion of slavery into the territories, not the issue of slavery per se—that will lead to the Civil War.

The Republican Party is a totally sectional party. It appeals only to northerners, but the northern population is so much greater than the southern population that Abraham Lincoln is able to win the presidency in 1860 with only northern votes. He is able to win the electoral college. This is only the second presidential campaign that the Republican Party runs, and it wins. Keep in mind, though, that Lincoln did not receive a majority of the popular vote, only a plurality. He did receive a majority of the electoral college [votes]. His election led directly to secession of the Deep South and, very soon thereafter, to civil war. That civil war called into question not simply future U.S. power in the hemisphere and the world but the continued existence of the nation.

Southern diplomacy focused on obtaining British and French recognition and aid. If successful, that recognition and aid could be as important in ensuring Confederate independence as French recognition and aid had been in ensuring American independence during the Revolutionary War. Britain and France had numerous reasons to support the southern states, [including] fear of the Yankee colossus—a permanently divided United States is far less of a threat to British and French possessions and interests in the Western Hemisphere. In addition to that, the British fear the high protective tariffs that northern industrialists want passed and that the Republican Party will put into effect. For the French (under the rule of Napoleon III), Napoleon III wants to conquer Mexico, and he needs to negate any effective opposition by the United States to this move. Most important, the British economy is dependent upon southern cotton, what is known as "King Cotton." The textile industry is the biggest industry in England, and 75 percent of all British cotton exports come from the South. The textile industry employs between 4 and 5 million people, more than 20 percent of all British workers, and 20 percent of the entire British population depends directly or indirectly on the textile industry.

Knowing this, the South embargoed the sale of cotton in 1861 in order to force British and French recognition and intervention—what became known as "King Cotton Diplomacy." But the French will not act without British agreement. The British fleet still controls the high seas. Numerous factors argued against British recognition and intervention at this time. First, there was a huge surplus of cotton and cotton goods in 1861. The British did not need southern cotton at that point. What it did need were northern foodstuffs: wheat and corn. In addition, Britain had already abolished slavery within its empire, and given that empire, the British were loathe to support rebellion as a general principle. Furthermore, Lincoln's secretary of state, William Henry Seward, threatened war if Britain recognized or aided the Confederacy. The British feared for the future of Canada, as well as shipping losses. There was also an old European diplomatic tradition, which was that you recognized a government only when it had shown an ability to maintain its independence.

Looking at all of these factors, I would conclude that they are fairly equal. They are balanced. British behavior is thus going to depend, to a great extent, on military and political events taking place during the war. If the Confederate armies are successful, there is a very good chance that the British and French will intervene, which would guarantee southern independence.

In retrospect, the greatest possibility of European intervention occurred in 1861 and in 1862. On November 8, 1861, Captain Charles Wilkes of the USS *San Jacinto* stopped a British mail ship, the *Trent*, and seized two Confederate emissaries on their way to England: James Mason and John Slidell. The British were infuriated and issued an ultimatum: Release those two emissaries traveling under a British flag or else. Lincoln and Seward decided they had to back down. Lincoln's famous comment at the time was: "One war at a time, please." Furthermore, you needed British supplies for the Union army. But there's a role reversal here. Look back to Jefferson's embargo, the *Chesapeake* affair, the War of 1812, the impressment issue. There is a role reversal that has taken place here, which was noted by both Secretary of State Seward and Senator Charles Sumner of the Senate Foreign Relations Committee. The British have adopted our principles on impressment. We choose not to adopt theirs. This role reversal between the United States and Britain would actually reoccur many times during the Civil War. Since the United States was now the belligerent power and Britain the neutral power, 1812 is reversed. Britain, however, unlike the United States prior to 1812, will accede to the new U.S. definitions of neutral rights as more in line with its own definitions of neutral rights and will then use these during World War I.

The second major episode that could have led to British and French intervention occurred in 1862. The Confederates triumphed militarily in the eastern theater. They defeated George McClellan's invasion in the Peninsula Campaign. They then defeated his successor in the Second Battle of Bull Run. General Robert E. Lee is on a roll, if you will, and that led British Prime Minister Lord Palmerston and Foreign Minister Lord Russell to seriously consider a mediation offer that would have led to British recognition of southern independence.

But Palmerston decided to await the outcome of Lee's first invasion of the North, an invasion that ended with the bloodiest single day of the war at Antietam Creek in Maryland on September 17, 1862.

There were 23,000 casualties on that day. Tactically, the battle was a draw, but Lee was forced to leave the battlefield, leave Maryland, withdraw back into the South, and end his invasion of the North. He had been attacking. His orders had been discovered, and by the time the battle took place, Lee was on the defensive. He held the Union armies off, but he had to leave the field. It's a tactical draw, but with Lee's withdrawal, it looks like a victory compared to the Union defeats that had taken place previously.

It thus provides Abraham Lincoln with an opportunity, on September 22, 1862, to announce the Emancipation Proclamation, a proclamation that would go into effect on January 1, 1863. The Emancipation Proclamation is subject to a great deal of mythology. On September 22 and again on January 1, it didn't free anybody. What it said was that in areas still under the control of the Confederacy and in a state of rebellion on January 1, 1863, the slaves shall be considered free. But, of course, those areas are occupied by the Confederate army, so you cannot free those slaves at that particular time, though eventually it will. But much more important is the Thirteenth Amendment abolishing slavery. What it does at that moment is make British intervention much less likely. Lincoln turns the war into a war against slavery, not just a war for preservation of the Union, and that will have an impact on British public opinion.

In late October and early November of 1862, a deeply divided British government decides against a mediation offer that would have involved recognition of the South. The strongest voice against war came from the secretary for war, George Lewis. Those in favor of intervention included the foreign minister and others, but the cabinet sided with the secretary for war. Never again would the British come so close to intervening. Union military victories in 1863—most notably, at Gettysburg and at Vicksburg—followed by more victories in 1864 end any realistic possibility of European intervention in the war. That is in hindsight.

Additional crises did erupt during those years over the building of blockade runners, commerce raiders, and so-called "rams" for the Confederacy in Liverpool. This was a violation of British neutrality laws, but the way the Liverpool shipbuilders got around this was to build the ships but arm them elsewhere. Thereby, they technically avoided violating the British neutrality proclamation. The Union protested furiously. A diplomatic rupture was avoided through astute diplomacy on both sides. The Union's minister in London, Charles Francis Adams—son of John Quincy Adams, grandson of John Adams, and a brilliant diplomat—protested fiercely, especially over the release of the commerce raider the *Alabama* and the Laird rams, steam-powered warships with heavy armor that would wreak havoc on Union ships. Adams actually threatened war, which was a reversal of a previous role. Seward would be the one to constantly threaten war, and Adams would be the good cop in this good cop/bad cop routine that Seward and Adams pressed upon the British. Now Adams became a bad cop, as well. The British would detain the rams in 1863. The *Alabama*, however, and other commerce raiders would escape, and they would wreak havoc on Union shipping.

The ensuing American claims for damages caused by the *Alabama* and other ships built in the United Kingdom would disrupt Anglo-American relations for years after the Civil War. Senator Sumner claimed that Britain owed the United States the extraordinary 19th-century sum of more than $2 billion on the grounds that those commerce raiders and rams had extended the war for two years, and therefore, Britain needed to pay the cost of the war for those last two years. Obviously, even the British treasury could not afford that amount of money. Some said: "Well, then you can cede Canada to us to pay off the debt." The issue was finally resolved in 1871 in the Treaty of Washington, whereby the British expressed regret for what had happened and agreed to a tribunal in Geneva to determine damages and claims. The British would eventually pay $15.5 million to settle this issue.

The Confederate failure to obtain British and French recognition and intervention was a major factor in the eventual defeat of the South. That defeat, in turn, guaranteed continued U.S. dominance in the Western Hemisphere as a large, single, powerful entity, one that now had experience in total war and an ensuing military tradition that it would use in both World War I and World War II.

The war also marked the triumph of northern industry over the agrarian South and guaranteed continued industrial growth. With that growth would come emerging status as a great power and a more centralized government, at that. In fact, it is in the Civil War that the United States shifts from the plural verb "the United States *are*" to the [singular] verb "the United States *is*," denoting this centralization, this unification that had taken place and, very soon, the great-power status that [would] take place. Seward would illustrate that status immediately after the Civil War, when he forced the French out of Mexico (or appeared to force the French out of Mexico).

During the Civil War, Britain, France, and Spain had all intervened militarily in Mexico at the port of Veracruz, when Mexico had defaulted on its debts. The British and Spanish soon withdrew, but Napoleon kept his army there. By 1863, he had succeeded in conquering Mexico City and installing the younger brother of the Austrian emperor, Ferdinand Maximilian, as emperor of Mexico, supported by a French army. Seward made clear his opposition to this violation of the Monroe Doctrine, but obviously, he was powerless during the Civil War to act. In 1865, however, with the Civil War at an end, Seward increased his diplomatic protests to Paris and sent substantial troops down to the Mexican border. Gradually, he ratcheted up the pressure. By early 1866, he demands a French military withdrawal. He also moves to block any Austrian intervention. Napoleon III withdraws his troops. Subsequently, Maximilian will be executed, and Mexico will regain its independence.

Some historians credit this primarily to Mexican guerilla warfare and European preoccupations at the time, not to Seward. Particularly, it is at this time that you have the rise of Prussia and Bismarck's wars of unification that will eventually form Germany. These are beginning to take place now, but other historians argue that it is Seward's pressure that forced the French to back down and the Austrians to back down, and that, in doing so, Seward successfully illustrated that the United States had obtained great-power status. It had forced another great power, France, to back down with the threat of military action.

Whether or not Seward and the United States had achieved this great-power status by 1866, the combination of Union victory in the Civil War and the enormous expansion of American industry that would now take place would give the United States very clearly that status by the 1890s. It is to that time period that we must now turn.

Lecture Ten
The "New Empire" of Overseas Imperialism

Scope:

Between 1865 and 1898, the United States appeared to enter a "dark age" of virtually no expansion or even diplomacy, followed by an extraordinary burst of expansion that focused on a war with Spain in 1898 and the ensuing acquisition of a formal overseas empire. In reality, however, the post–Civil War years witnessed an explosion of American industry that made the United States the largest economic power in the world by the 1890s. That explosive growth provided the power and prompted the desire to obtain an overseas empire, a desire acted on long before the events of 1898. This lecture will examine these early efforts at overseas expansion, particularly in Hawaii and the Caribbean, as well as the causes and consequences of the 1898 war with Spain that resulted in the acquisition of a formal colonial empire.

Outline

I. Although the United States made few formal territorial acquisitions in the 50-year period following the war with Mexico, it clearly established during that time the foundations for the burst of overseas expansion and influence that would occur in the late 19th and early 20th centuries.

  A. As noted in the last lecture, Americans during the 1850s attempted to expand and establish major influence in Central America and the Caribbean.

  B. Simultaneously, William Henry Seward envisioned a "new empire" for the United States that would encompass all of North America and expand into South America, the Pacific, and Asia.

    1. As secretary of state from 1861–1869, Seward attempted numerous territorial acquisitions in fulfillment of this vision but was thwarted in most of them by the Civil War, Reconstruction, and a reluctant Congress.

    2. His one great success was the purchase of Alaska from Russia in 1867, a purchase he saw as furthering both territorial expansion over North America and commercial expansion to Asia and the Pacific.

C. Such expansion would not culminate for another three decades, but during those years, an enormous burst of industrial growth made the United States the greatest economic power in the world.

    1. That growth would provide the United States with the economic and military power it needed to participate successfully with other great powers in an age of global imperial expansion and competition.

    2. It would also fuel the desire of the United States to expand overseas in order to obtain new markets for the nation's surplus goods, protection against European encroachments in its sphere of influence, and international prestige and recognition of its status as a world power.

II. The years 1889–1898 witnessed an intellectual reformulation, a major expansion of the U.S. Navy, and a series of international crises that set the stage for the war and imperial expansion that would follow in 1898–1899.

A. The intellectual reformulation focused on the need for expansion overseas to provide a new frontier and fulfill the unique American mission, as well as prevent a loss of liberty at home. Leading figures in this reformulation included Frederick Jackson Turner, Josiah Strong, Brooks Adams, and Alfred Thayer Mahan.

B. Mahan's theories of sea power provided military and geopolitical rationales for the creation of the large naval force that would be needed for overseas expansion.

C. The depression of 1893 gave added impetus for overseas expansion and fostered a sense of urgency and "psychic crisis."

D. In the international sphere, Americans living in Hawaii took over the government, declared a republic, and requested annexation to the United States in the early 1890s.

E. Simultaneously, the United States almost went to war with Britain when Washington demanded the right to arbitrate a boundary dispute between British Guiana and Venezuela.

    1. Britain's eventual agreement to American arbitration clearly illustrated the growth in U.S. power that had occurred by this time.

2. It also served as the foundation for an expansion of the Monroe Doctrine by Secretary of State Richard Olney, who boldly asserted American power.

III. All this "muscle-flexing" reached a crescendo in 1898 when the United States went to war with Spain over Cuba.

   A. Contrary to popular mythology, the United States did not go to war to help free the Cuban people from Spanish tyranny and atrocities (as reported and distorted by the "yellow press"), to respond to the insult of the notorious De Lôme letter, or to avenge the destruction of the USS *Maine*.

   B. Rather, Washington demanded that Spain end the chaos and devastation on the island by successfully suppressing the rebellion that had broken out in 1895 or by acceding to rebel demands; by 1898, Washington insisted that Spain agree to U.S. arbitration.

   C. Along with the anti-autonomy riots of early 1898, the De Lôme letter and destruction of the *Maine* were key events in President McKinley's (1843–1901) decision to go to war. These developments offered evidence of Spanish insincerity in negotiations and Spain's inability to control the situation in Cuba.

   D. The United States quickly achieved military victory over the Spanish in this "Splendid Little War," but in the process, McKinley decided to keep the Spanish colonies in the Pacific and the Caribbean that his forces had conquered and obtain congressional approval for the formal annexation of Hawaii.

   E. After bitter debate regarding this apparent break with American tradition via acquisition of a formal overseas colonial empire, the United States first annexed Hawaii and then, in the Treaty of Paris, obtained the Philippines, Guam, and Puerto Rico.

   F. One of the reasons McKinley sought to acquire a formal colonial empire was a series of events then taking place in China. As we will see in the next lecture, McKinley and his successors would create an informal overseas empire to parallel the formal one acquired in the wake of the Spanish-American War.

Suggested Readings:

Beisner, *From the Old Diplomacy to the New, 1865–1900.*

Campbell, *The Transformation of American Foreign Relations, 1865–1900.*

Kennedy, *The Rise and Fall of the Great Powers.*

LaFeber, *The New Empire.*

Questions to Consider:

1. What were the most important factors in the emergence of the United States as a great power between 1865 and 1899?

2. Why did the United States decide to acquire a formal overseas colonial empire in the late 19th century despite its anti-colonial origins and traditions?

Lecture Ten—Transcript
The "New Empire" of Overseas Imperialism

The United States would make very few formal territorial acquisitions between 1865 and 1898. Indeed, foreign affairs in general went into a period of deep decline, with the era often referred to as the "Dark Ages" of American foreign and military policies. The army would be cut down to 25,000 after the Civil War. The navy would simply be allowed to rot away. The era became known for massive corruption and incompetence in both foreign and domestic affairs. Indeed, foreign policy became largely a domestic political football.

There [was] a series of international crises and near wars, but they are over rather humorous and rather meaningless issues. One of my favorites occurred on October 16, 1891, the so-called *Baltimore* affair, where soldiers from the USS *Baltimore* were in the True Blue Saloon in Valparaiso, Chile, when a riot broke out. Two U.S. sailors were killed, 17 injured. U.S. President Benjamin Harrison demanded an apology from Chile and threatened a diplomatic rupture and war. In the ensuing controversy, the question arose: Were the American sailors drunk? The captain of the *Baltimore* said, "No, they were sober." But Captain Evans of the USS *Yorktown*, which had been sent to Valparaiso, disagreed and later wrote: "His men were probably drunk on shore, properly drunk; they went ashore, many of them, for the purpose of getting drunk; which they did on Chilean rum paid for with good United States money. When in this condition," Captain Evans argued, "they were more entitled to protection than if they had been sober." An interesting argument.

Perhaps most telling about this time period is this: How many presidents or secretaries of state between 1865 and 1898 can you name? They are two lists of nonentities for the most part. The presidents: Johnson, Grant, Rutherford B. Hayes, James Garfield, Chester Arthur, Grover Cleveland, Benjamin Harrison, Grover Cleveland again, and then William McKinley. The secretaries of state—the first and last ones should be noticeable, as they're quite important. William Henry Seward was the first and John Hay was the last, but in between there were: Hamilton Fish; William Evarts; James G. Blaine, who was important—the "Plumed Knight," James G. Blaine of Maine; Theodore Frelinghuysen; Thomas Bayard; Blaine again; then John Foster; Walter Gresham; Richard Olney, whom we will be talking about extensively in this lecture; John Sherman; William Day; and John Hay.

Despite this list of apparent nonentities, the United States during these years clearly established the foundations for the burst of overseas expansion and influence that would occur in the late 19th and early 20th centuries. Indeed, it had all begun even earlier. As previously noted in two past lectures, Americans had developed a very strong interest in China, Hawaii, and Japan well before the Civil War, as well as in Central America and the Caribbean.

During and immediately after the Civil War, Secretary of State William Henry Seward would attempt to revive U.S. territorial expansion, as well as commercial expansion, and create a "new empire" for the United States, one that would encompass not only the rest of North America, the old territorial dream, but also South America. He talked about both Mexico City and St. Paul, Minnesota, as capitals of this new, expanded entity, and the country would then expand commercially across the Pacific to Asia. San Francisco, he argued, was to be the "Constantinople" of this new American empire, an empire that would require a new navy, a Central American canal, and island bases in the Caribbean and the Pacific Ocean. As secretary of state during and after the Civil War, Seward attempted numerous territorial acquisitions in fulfillment of this vision. He would attempt to purchase—believe it or not—all or parts of the Danish West Indies, Santo Domingo, Haiti, Puerto Rico, St. Bartholomew, St. Pierre, Martinique, Cuba, Tiger Island, Greenland, Iceland, Hawaii, Borneo, the Fiji Islands, Midway, and Alaska. His enemies labeled him a megalomaniac who saw himself as the personal instrument of Manifest Destiny. He would be thwarted in most of his efforts—first, by the Civil War and, then, by Reconstruction and a Congress reluctant to agree, given the tasks ahead of it. His one great success was the purchase of Alaska from Russia in 1867, when the Russians decided to sell it for $7.2 million. Even that was a near thing, and historians have discovered there was massive bribery of congressmen and senators to get even this through.

Seward was a pivotal player, though, particularly if you look at Alaska. Alaska was different from previous territorial acquisitions. It was not contiguous with the rest of the United States. There were no U.S. citizens in Alaska. There were no demands for annexation by people living there or anywhere, and there was no provision for eventual statehood. Alaska was purchased as a colony. Seward saw all of this as temporary, with the purchase furthering both continued territorial expansion over North America and commercial expansion to Asia and the Pacific. It would further territorial expansion by creating a sandwich, by creating two slices of bread; in between, one found British Columbia. This would eventually lead to the annexation of British Columbia and the rest of Canada. Meanwhile, the Aleutian Islands would serve as a drawbridge to Asia, with the Alaskan timber resources available to create a great merchant marine and navy. When asked in his later years his greatest contribution, Seward said it was the purchase of Alaska, but it would take his countrymen a generation to figure that out.

Seward was way ahead of his time. Overseas territorial expansion would not culminate for another three decades, but during the post–Civil War years, there was an enormous burst of economic growth in both industry and agriculture that would make the United States the greatest economic power in the world. Just a few statistics here: Between 1865 and 1898, wheat production increased 256 percent; corn, 222 percent; refined sugar, 460 percent; coal, 800 percent; steel rails, 523 percent; miles of railroad track in operation, over 567 percent; petroleum production went from 3 million barrels to 55 million barrels; steel ingots and castings, from less than 20,000 long tons to nearly 9 million.

The United States became the greatest industrial and economic power in the world by the mid-1890s. Indeed, by 1914, its industrial output in key areas—coal, pig iron, and steel—was as great [as] or greater than that of most of the other great powers put together. Both A. J. P. Taylor and Paul Kennedy, British and U.S. historians, have commented that the United States was not simply a rival country; it was a rival continent.

This growth would provide the United States with, first, the economic power and, eventually, the military power that it needed to compete successfully with other great powers in an era of global imperial expansion and competition. Paul Kennedy rates U.S. economic growth in his great book *The Rise and Fall of the Great Powers* as the most decisive change in the global balance of power during the entire era. But Kennedy also notes that the United States underspent militarily. Less than 1 percent of America's gross national product went to the army and navy at this time. Indeed, Kennedy has argued that rising powers tend to underspend militarily, whereas declining powers tend to overspend militarily in a desperate attempt to defend their entire empire when they no longer have the economic capacity to do so—a theme we will be coming back to later in this course.

The enormous economic growth of the United States would also provide the desire or perceived need, depending upon whom you look at, to expand overseas in order to obtain new markets for its surplus goods, protection against European encroachments in its sphere of influence, as well as international prestige and recognition by others of its status as a world power. That perceived need was tremendously reinforced by the fact that American economic growth after the Civil War was not steady. Instead, it was marked by very sharp swings in the business cycle. Instead of a straight line going up, what you have is a wave—periodic depressions, boom-and-bust cycles—depressions from 1873 to 1878 and again in 1893 to 1897. These, in turn, led to major and violent conflicts between industrial workers and management. They also led to revolt in the agrarian sector of the economy [by angry farmers]; the major populist movement at this time, culminating in the Populist Party; and a growing belief in the country as a whole that overseas expansion was necessary not only to save the economy but to save the entire American character and political system, as well.

All of this would culminate in 1898 and 1899, but in the preceding decade, the 1890s, you would see a critical set of precursors to what would occur in 1898 and 1899—earlier on in the decade, a major intellectual reformulation, a major expansion of the U.S. Navy, and a series of international crises—all of which clearly set the stage for the war and the imperial expansion that would follow in 1898. A key component of the intellectual reformulation was the growing belief that the United States needed to find a new overseas frontier. In 1890, the Bureau of the Census announced that the frontier no longer existed, that it could not find a line separating white settlement from wilderness—Native Americans, whatever, in different eras, it would be called.

Three years later, a young historian from Wisconsin, Frederick Jackson Turner, would enunciate his famous "frontier" interpretation of American history. Turner would argue that the existence of the frontier had been the dynamic of a unique American character and a unique American history—that individualism, democracy, fluid social structure, and prosperity all flowed from the frontier. With the end of the frontier, Turner argued, this first period of American history had ended. The clear implication of Turner's thesis is that the openness of American society had been linked to an open frontier and that the United States must find a new frontier or else become just like the monarchial powers of Europe.

Turner was not read by the public at large. He was read primarily by other historians, but that group included such individuals as Theodore Roosevelt and Woodrow Wilson. More importantly, however, Turner summarized and verbalized what many Americans were thinking. That thought pattern was reinforced by the major economic depression that hit in that same year, 1893, and the extensive labor strife of the era. [There were] hundreds and then thousands of major work stoppages, many of them violent. The fear grew that the economy and the entire American dream were collapsing with the end of the frontier. But the new frontier needed to be more than just an economic frontier. What you see here is a rebirth of the old American mission concept—in terms that the British writer at this time Rudyard Kipling would label the "White Man's Burden"—the mission to bring Christianity and Western "civilization" to the supposed "backward" peoples of Asia and Africa. This was, in turn, linked to social Darwinism. The scientific racism of the 1840s had now grown into social Darwinism, using Darwinian concepts of natural selection and "survival of the fittest" as applied to entire nations and entire cultures.

In this country, it was best illustrated in the writings of the U.S. missionary Josiah Strong, who argued for the racial superiority of Anglo-Saxons based on their fusion of Christianity and civil liberty, along with their genius for money-making and for colonizing. By the principles of social Darwinism, Anglo-Saxons must expand and spread these ideas or they will die. This was survival of the fittest, with China to be the great future battleground.

Similarly, Brooks Adams, another member of the famous Adams family, in *The Law of Civilization and Decay*, came up with an apocalyptic vision of history in which he argued that U.S. society was in decline because individual greed had overcome all other values. This process could be reversed if a new national spirit arose

[and] if the national spirit could be recaptured via overseas expansion. What some argued was that what this country needs is a good war.

Theodore Roosevelt would be a key figure in this emerging worldview, what one scholar labeled the "warrior critique of business civilization." Roosevelt represented a new generation of young, intensely nationalistic and imperialistic political figures. But it was not simply people like Roosevelt who wanted war. The philosopher William James argued for the moral equivalent of war (James was a pacifist)—the idea of something to stop the emphasis on simple greed, simple money-making, to bring the nation together in a new national cause.

Naval captain Alfred Thayer Mahan would, during this era, provide the key strategic concepts for this new imperialist worldview in his influential 1890 book *The Influence of Sea Power in History* and in other later writings. Mahan would argue that sea power was the key to national greatness, and he would cite British history as the key example in this regard. Mahan held a neo-mercantilist view of shipping and commerce as key, with naval force needed to protect and expand shipping and commerce, for a nation to be great. The oceans, he argued, were not moats protecting the United States; they were great highways. He asked Americans to change their views of the oceans in this regard. Overseas colonies, Mahan argued, were needed as protective markets and for naval bases and coaling stations for the fleet that he wished to build. A canal through Central America was also needed in order to keep the fleet concentrated. Mahan's great principle of naval warfare was concentration of force. You never divide the fleet; you keep its firepower concentrated in a single battleship fleet. A canal was also needed, he argued, to provide a new short commercial route to Asia that the United States could use.

It is far from accidental, in this regard, that the ensuing U.S. empire, both the formal empire and—as we will see—the informal empire, would focus on canal routes in Central America, islands in the Caribbean to provide naval bases and to protect the approaches to any canal, and islands in the Pacific to provide naval bases en route to China. As we will see in the next two lectures, all of American expansion fit into this pattern. Mahan's theories would provide the rationale for the creation of the large naval power that would be needed for overseas expansion.

In 1880, the United States Navy ranked 17th in the world behind Chile. There were still 1,942 ships left over from the Civil War, but only 48 were capable of even firing a gun. In Oscar Wilde's famous book *The Canterville Ghost*, in this volume, the Canterville ghost had an interesting comment back to a young American lady who complained that her country had no ruins and no curiosities. "No ruins! No curiosities!" the ghost replied, "you have your Navy and your manners!"

In 1893, the U.S. Navy had risen from 17th ranking in 1880 up to 7th rank, and it was rising. The key figure here was President Benjamin Harrison's secretary of the Navy, Benjamin Franklin Tracy. "The sea will be the future seat of empire," Tracy wrote, "and we shall rule it as certainly as the sun doth rise."

The depression of 1893 provided added impetus for overseas expansion, as well as a sense of urgency and what historian Richard Hofstadter labeled "a psychic crisis." In the midst of this worst depression in all of American history, Americans—frustrated, feeling helpless—chose to lash out at others. You had a growing American belligerency in the international arena.

You could see this in numerous areas. In Hawaii, aided by the United States minister and U.S. Marines from the USS *Boston*, Americans living in Hawaii overthrew the native Queen Liliuokalani, or Queen Lil, in 1893; declared a republic; and requested annexation by the United States President Benjamin Harrison favored this, but when the new president, Grover Cleveland, examined it and saw the involvement of the U.S. minister and the Marines, he withdrew the annexation treaty. It would not be revived again until 1898.

In 1895, the United States almost went to war with Britain when Washington demanded the right to arbitrate a boundary dispute between British Guiana and Venezuela. Britain's eventual agreement to this clearly illustrated the growth in American power that had occurred by this time. It also provided a corollary to an expansion of the Monroe Doctrine by the secretary of state, Richard Olney, who very boldly asserted American power. Let me quote you one paragraph from Richard Olney's message to the British:

Today the United States is practically sovereign on this continent, and its fiat is law upon the subjects to which it confines its interposition. Why? It is not because of the pure friendship or goodwill felt for it. It is not simply by reason of its high character as a civilized state, nor because wisdom and justice and equity are the invariable characteristics of the dealings of the United States. It is because, in addition to all other grounds, its infinite resources combined with its isolated position render it master of the situation and practically invulnerable as against any or all other powers.

Using such logic, Olney demanded of the greatest empire in the world that it allow the United States to arbitrate a dispute, and the British knuckled under. All of this "muscle-flexing" would reach a crescendo in 1898. The United States did not go to war with Britain; it did go to war with Spain in 1898 over Cuba. According to popular belief, the United States went to war essentially for the following reasons: [first,] to help free the Cuban people from Spanish tyranny and Spanish atrocities, atrocities that had been reported and distorted by the so-called "Yellow Press" [and] which inflamed public opinion. There was a newspaper war going on between Pulitzer and Hearst in which they tried to outdo each other in atrocity stories, many of which were invented. Supposedly, the United States also went to war to respond to the insult of the notorious De Lôme letter, in which the Spanish ambassador to the United States, [Enrique] Dupuy de Lôme, had insulted President McKinley by calling him "weak and a bidder for the admiration of the crowd, besides being a would-be politician who tries to leave a door open behind himself while keeping on good terms with the jingoes of his party." The final reason, supposedly, [was] to avenge the destruction of the USS *Maine* in Havana harbor in February of 1898, with the battle cry "Remember the *Maine*!"

Reality was a bit more complex. Ever since the latest rebellion in Cuba had begun in 1895, Washington had demanded that Spain end the chaos and devastation on the island in one of two ways: Either suppress the rebellion or accede to the demands of the rebels. Spain had done neither. A bloody military stalemate had ensued. By the beginning of 1898, Washington, under William McKinley, was demanding that Spain agree to U.S. arbitration—very similar to the way it had insisted three years earlier, under a Democratic president, Grover Cleveland, and his secretary of state, Richard Olney, that

Britain submit to such arbitration over the Venezuelan boundary dispute—but Spain refused. It did announce an autonomy plan for Cuba, but that plan was rejected by the rebels, and Spanish soldiers in Cuba led riots against it.

It was those riots that led to the sending of the USS *Maine* to Havana harbor. [They] also led to the De Lôme letter and the destruction of the *Maine*. These were, of course, key events in McKinley's decision to go to war, but why? It was not simply because the public demanded war, although it did; 1898 was a congressional election year, and McKinley was under tremendous pressure from his own party, as well as the public in general. But equally if not more important, what happened with the De Lôme letter and the *Maine* provided evidence of Spanish insincerity in negotiations and an inability to control the situation in Cuba. The *Maine*, as a warship in harbor, was officially under the protection of the Spanish government; it was supposed to be. How could this have happened? The public may have thought the Spaniards did it, but the administration knew better. The Spaniards would be the last people in the world to do it. Indeed, in reality, the *Maine* blew up not because of the Spanish attack, not because of lack of control, but instead because of defective engineering within the warship.

In the 1970s, Admiral Hyman Rickover of the U.S. Navy ordered a new study of the *Maine*. The conclusion, in all likelihood, was that the Maine blew up not because of an external explosion but because of an internal explosion that began with spontaneous combustion in the coal bunker, which then blew up a nearby powder magazine. This had happened in another ship, but the spontaneous combustion and fire had been put out before it blew up the ship. It is a classic example of perception versus reality and why perception is often more important than reality within history.

With the battle cry "Remember the *Maine*," the United States went to war and very quickly achieved military victory over Spanish forces in what was labeled the "Splendid Little War"—first via Admiral Dewey's destruction of the Spanish fleet in the Philippines, then in Cuba, and then Puerto Rico in the Caribbean. But McKinley, as the war ended and the Spanish sued for an armistice, decided on peace terms that went far beyond the original war aim. The original war aim had been the independence of Cuba. McKinley now decided to keep the Philippines and Puerto Rico, areas that his forces had conquered, as well as force the Spanish to give the United States a base in the Marianas, the island of Guam.

Why did he do this? He told a group of ministers the following:

> When I ... realized that the Philippines had dropped into our laps, I confess I did not know what to do with them. I sought counsel from all sides ... but got little help. I thought first we would take only Manila; then Luzon; then other islands perhaps also. I walked the floor of the White House night after night until midnight, and I am not ashamed to tell you, gentlemen, that I went down on my knees and prayed to Almighty God for light and guidance more than one night. And one night late, it came to me this way—I don't know how it was, but it came: (1) That we could not give them back to Spain—that would be cowardly and dishonorable; (2) [that] we could not turn them over to France and Germany—our commercial rivals in the Orient—that would be bad business and discreditable; (3) [that] we could not leave them to themselves—they were unfit for self-government—and they would soon have anarchy and misrule over there, worse than Spain's was; and (4) that there was nothing left for us to do but to take them all, and to educate the Filipinos and uplift and civilize and Christianize them, and by God's grace do the very best that we could by them, as our fellow-men for whom Christ also died.

That was a very nice story, which conveniently forgets that the Filipinos had been Catholic for approximately 400 years. Whatever the true reason, Spain was forced to agree in the Treaty of Paris. McKinley also pressed Congress during the war to annex Hawaii as well, thereby establishing an overseas colonial empire in the Caribbean and across the Pacific that now included American forces in occupation of Cuba, Puerto Rico, Hawaii, Guam, and the Philippines. Numerous Americans would object vehemently to this apparent break with American tradition via the acquisition of a formal overseas colonial empire. The United States had always expanded, but it had always incorporated areas unto itself. Now, it was to have formal colonies, and we had been born of an anti-colonial revolution. After bitter debate, the Senate finally ratified the treaty in 1899 by the very close vote of 57 to 27. The United States became a formal colonial power with an overseas empire.

One of the major reasons McKinley decided to obtain a formal colonial empire was the series of events then taking place in China. Discussion of those events, in turn, then brings us to the informal overseas empire that McKinley and his successors would create to parallel the formal one. It is to that informal empire that we will now turn.

Lecture Eleven
Informal Empire—Roosevelt to Wilson

Scope:

Whereas President William McKinley established a formal empire during and after the 1898 war with Spain, his three successors established a related but informal empire in Central America and the Caribbean. That informal empire took the form of U.S. economic dominance throughout the region; the creation of an independent Republic of Panama as a site for a transoceanic canal; protectorate treaties with that new nation, as well as Cuba, Nicaragua, Haiti, and the Dominican Republic, that provided for both American military intervention and financial supervision; and a new corollary to the Monroe Doctrine to justify this behavior. The informal imperialism of the United States also involved major military interventions in Mexico that almost led to another full-scale war between the two nations. This lecture explains how and why this informal empire was created, specifically exploring the actions of the supposedly anti-imperialist Woodrow Wilson, as well as the openly imperialist Theodore Roosevelt and William Howard Taft.

Outline

I. The acquisition of a formal overseas empire led to a massive debate in the Senate and the public at large.

   A. Those favoring a formal overseas empire won the Senate debate over ratification of the Treaty of Paris in 1899.

   B. The Philippine insurrection and U.S. military tactics in suppressing that insurrection led to renewed debate and congressional investigations and turned many Americans against additional overseas colonial acquisitions.

II. The informal American empire was based primarily on trade and U.S. economic power.

   A. Even before the war with Spain, Americans had extended their massive economic and financial power into Central America, the Caribbean, the Pacific, and Asia.

B. Major hopes for future trade expansion focused on China, the greatest untapped market in the world but one that the European imperialist powers appeared ready to carve up by 1898.

C. One reason for acquiring a colonial empire in the Pacific had been the desire to establish a series of naval bases from the United States to China to prevent such a partition.

D. In 1899, Secretary of State John Hay (1838–1905) issued the famous Open Door Notes regarding China.

    1. These notes affirmed U.S. policies that had actually been in effect for nearly 50 years, but with this official issuance, those policies became virtually canonized.

    2. They also became, according to some scholars, the model for the expansion of U.S. power and influence globally.

III. In the aftermath of the war with Spain, expansion over the next two decades focused on Central America and the Caribbean.

A. The United States desired control of this area for a host of strategic, economic, diplomatic, and ideological reasons, most notably, the desire to build a transoceanic canal and to control the strategic approaches to that canal.

B. The primary method for gaining informal control was the creation of five protectorates in the area between 1901 and 1915: Cuba, Panama, Nicaragua, Haiti, and the Dominican Republic. Each of these small nations would officially remain independent but would be subject to U.S. economic and financial control and U.S. military intervention under certain circumstances.

C. Cuba was the first protectorate to be established and, thus, the model in this regard via the terms of the Platt Amendment of 1901.

    1. The Cubans agreed not to incur debt beyond their means or do anything else that would allow another foreign power to obtain control and to allow both U.S. military intervention to enforce these terms and a sanitation program to wipe out yellow fever.

2. A year later, a trade treaty allowed Cuban sugar lower U.S. tariff rates—a boon to the Cuban sugar industry but a move that made that industry, and the Cuban economy, more dependent on the United States.

3. In 1906, President Theodore Roosevelt (1858–1919) ordered U.S. troops back into Cuba to end a revolution and civil war that had broken out.

D. Roosevelt also moved to build a transoceanic canal during his presidency, which led to the creation of the Republic of Panama and a second protectorate.

1. A province of Colombia, Panama was one of two potential routes for such a canal and the site of an earlier canal effort that had failed, organized by a French engineer, Ferdinand de Lesseps.

2. Congress had at first favored the alternative route through Nicaragua, but investors in the old Panama Canal Company convinced both Roosevelt and Congress to negotiate with Colombia for the Panama route via treaty instead.

3. When the Colombian government rejected the treaty and demanded more money, the investors organized a revolution and a new government, which Roosevelt supported and quickly recognized. A 1903 treaty gave the United States the rights to a canal zone through Panama—and the right to intervene militarily to protect it.

E. Roosevelt also provided the official rationale for such military interventions with his famous corollary to the Monroe Doctrine.

1. According to Roosevelt, European nations had a right to collect unpaid debts in the Caribbean and Central America by force, but such action could violate the Monroe Doctrine. Under Roosevelt's corollary, the United States would intervene for the Europeans, militarily as well as financially, to make sure the debts were paid.

2. By this corollary and his specific actions, Roosevelt played a major role in turning the Caribbean into an American lake.

IV. A larger number of U.S. financial and military interventions would occur under Roosevelt's successors, William Howard Taft (1857–1930) and Woodrow Wilson (1856–1924).

   A. Taft preferred "dollar diplomacy" to Roosevelt's military interventions, while the moralistic and anti-imperialistic Wilson opposed both and promised a major shift in Latin American policy. But Taft would send U.S. troops into Nicaragua and establish financial supervision of that nation between 1909 and 1912, while Wilson would send troops into Haiti and the Dominican Republic, establish financial supervision over the former, and continue financial and military supervision in the other protectorates.

   B. This discrepancy can be partially explained by the existence of the canal, which needed to be defended, and by the fact that Taft and Wilson shared Roosevelt's desire for control, order, and stability in the area as one way to prevent European intervention.

   C. An additional factor for Wilson was his desire to spread democracy into the area—even if it involved the use of force.

   1. Wilson's first intervention in the Mexican Revolution in 1913–1914 was an effort to overthrow the military dictator Victoriano Huerta, who had overthrown and murdered the constitutionalist reformer Francisco Madero.

   2. This effort alienated all parties in Mexico, though it did aid in Huerta's overthrow by Venustiano Carranza and Pancho Villa, two of Madero's lieutenants.

   3. Carranza and Villa then fought for control of the country. When a defeated Villa attacked Americans on both sides of the border, Wilson sent an army into Mexico that soon clashed with Carranza's forces and left the two nations on the verge of a full-scale war.

   4. War would be narrowly averted and the U.S. Army would be withdrawn, but the entire episode, as well as Wilson's other actions in Latin America, greatly expanded the informal American empire.

Suggested Readings:

Collin, *Theodore Roosevelt's Caribbean.*

Gilderhus, *Pan-American Visions.*

Healy, *Drive to Hegemony.*

McCormick, *China Market.*

Questions to Consider:

1. Critics have long charged that an Open Door/free trade policy constitutes "the imperialism of the strong." Do you agree? Why?

2. Compare and contrast the policies of Roosevelt, Taft, and Wilson in Central America and the Caribbean. What differences and similarities do you note?

Lecture Eleven—Transcript
Informal Empire—Roosevelt to Wilson

The formal overseas empire that the United States created in 1898 and 1899 led, as noted in the last lecture, to a massive debate in the country. Those opposed to this argued that it was against American tradition—we had been born from an anti-colonial revolt—that it was morally wrong, that it was a violation of the Constitution, that it would be a violation of U.S. principles and would destroy liberty at home. How could you maintain a tyrannical empire overseas and liberty at home? They argued that economically, it wasn't necessary, that the greatest untapped market in the world—China—was open. It was not worth the cost of administration. They also argued that racially, the Americans could not and should not admit these inferior, backward peoples who were incapable of self-government.

The imperialists had countered that the American tradition had always been expansionist; that isolationism was a dated concept; that technology and the new American navy made overseas areas contiguous; that it was morally correct, via the White Man's Burden and the American mission; that, indeed, it was immoral not to take these territories and "uplift them"; that you did not violate the Constitution; that you could maintain liberty at home while having an empire abroad; that, indeed, liberty at home would disappear without Far Eastern markets; that the colonies were necessary as coaling stations; and that racially, you would not have to admit these inferior peoples—you would keep them outside the temple of freedom, but you would tutor them.

The imperialists won the debate over the Treaty of Paris, but the debate would continue afterwards because the Filipinos, who had opposed Spanish rule, objected just as much to American rule. In 1899, under the leadership of Emilio Aguinaldo, they rebelled against the Americans. That rebellion would continue for many years and would cost thousands of American and Filipino lives before it was forcefully suppressed by the U.S. Army. The army would use brutal tactics in that suppression, including the notorious "water cure." Waterboarding, in this regard, is not all that new, just a different version. This would also lead to major congressional investigations and public criticism of the behavior of the army and the nation. As William James put it: "We are here for your own good; therefore unconditionally surrender to our tender mercies, or we'll blow you into kingdom come."

The Filipino insurrection would further sour the American people on the acquisition of additional colonial holdings. It would also lead to a pledge of eventual independence for the Philippines, a pledge that would be fulfilled in 1946. The era of formal empire building came to an end almost as quickly as it began. But informal, as opposed to formal, empire was another matter. Indeed, unlike the formal American empire, the informal empire that McKinley and his successors would create from 1898 to World War I aroused very little domestic opposition. Indeed, in many ways, it reflected a domestic consensus on how the United States should continue to expand its power and influence.

This informal empire was based primarily on trade and on American economic power. Even before the war with Spain, Americans had extended their massive economic and financial power into Central America and the Caribbean, where they came to dominate the economic life of many of these small countries. What was a small percentage of the American gross national product and American trade were huge percentages of the trade and economic life of these small countries. Americans had also extended this economic power into the Pacific and Asia. As previously mentioned, major hopes for future trade expansion had focused and continued to focus on China, the greatest untapped market in the world, millions upon millions of customers. But China was also weak. It was a decaying empire that European imperialist powers appeared ready to carve up by 1898. Indeed, it appeared that they had already begun to carve [it] up in the spheres of influence that they had established within China.

One reason for going to war with Spain in the spring of 1898 had been to get the Cuban crisis out of the way so that the McKinley administration could deal with this more serious crisis in Asia. One reason to obtain a colonial empire as a result of the war with Spain had been the desire to obtain a series of naval bases in the Pacific in order to prevent the partition of China. Again, look at the naval bases in the Pacific—going from Hawaii, to Guam, to the Philippines. Consequently, and again to prevent the partition, Secretary of State John Hay in 1899 and in 1900 issued his famous Open Door Notes regarding China.

The first note, issued on September 6, 1899, simply asked the great powers if they would agree to no trade discrimination within their spheres of influence on harbor or railroad fees. As the historian Thomas Bailey has quipped: "[This] was like asking all persons in a room who did not have thieving designs to stand up." Most of the great powers said they would agree if everyone else agreed. The Russians sent a veiled no. Hay announced that the answers were "final and definitive," which is an interesting way to obtain a foreign policy victory.

Hay's second note was issued on July 3, 1900, in response to the Boxer Uprising in China against foreigners. An intensely nationalistic movement, which many have labeled a xenophobic movement, had arisen in China, indirectly supported by the Chinese government. The Boxers laid siege to the foreign legations in Beijing and began to butcher converts and missionaries. All the great powers intervened militarily to stop this uprising, including the United States. Hay's fear, and that of others in Washington, was that these forces of the great powers would stay in China and carve that nation up. He therefore asserted in 1900 that American policy was to preserve the "territorial and administrative integrity" of China and to safeguard the principles of equal and impartial trade—not simply in the spheres of influence but in all of China.

These notes actually affirmed U.S. policies that had been in effect for China for nearly 50 years. Indeed, ever since the 1850s—some would argue the 1840s—these had been the essential principles of American policy vis-à-vis China. But with the official issuance of these Open Door Notes, those policies became virtually canonized. Ironically, the British, who had been the previous supporters of the Open Door, had asked for American support, given the crisis, in March of 1898. McKinley had turned the British down on the grounds of having to deal with the crisis with Spain. But now that that crisis was over, the Americans picked up the ball here.

Whether these notes actually played any major role in preventing the partition of China is open to serious question. Many scholars argue that China was not carved up simply because the great powers did not trust each other enough to peacefully carve up China and that, in effect, what you had was a balance of power here. But these notes were enormously popular in the United States and could be supported by both imperialists and anti-imperialists since they did not involve the taking of colonies.

The notes also became, according to some scholars, the model for the expansion of American power and influence globally throughout the 20th century. As William Appleman Williams and others have noted, the American policy was to keep potential markets open to an economic competition without any tariff barriers, an economic competition that the United States would win because of its enormous economic power. As the largest industrial power in the world, it could win any free and open competition. As Hay said, "We shall bring the sweat to their brows." In the process of winning that competition, the United States could remake traditional societies like China in the American image. With American goods would come American religion and American political values so that Christianity and democracy, as well as American goods, could influence China. But opposition to the carving up of China by the European imperial powers did not mean opposition to empire per se.

Indeed, as noted in the last lecture, the United States had created its own formal empire in the Pacific in the process of supposedly fighting to destroy the Spanish Empire in the Caribbean and free the Cuban people. In the two decades after the war with Spain, the United States also created a large informal empire in Central America and the Caribbean, as well.

Washington desired control of Central America and the Caribbean for a host of reasons: first, to keep the imperial European powers, most notably, a highly aggressive Germany, out of the area—defense of the Monroe Doctrine. The second reason was to maintain and expand the already massive and rapidly growing American trade and investments already in place within Latin America. The third reason was the old mission concept to promote democratic governments and humanitarian concerns in this area. But perhaps most importantly, by the turn of the century, [was] the desire to build a transoceanic canal in Central America for both economic and strategic reasons. [This] goes back to Alfred Thayer Mahan and [the idea of] economically creating a new, short, efficient route to the Far East to enable the concentrated U.S. fleet to move through a canal from one ocean to the other so that that fleet would never have to be divided.

Along with the desire to build such a canal went the desire to control the strategic approaches to any canal in the Caribbean. Although the United States had acquired Puerto Rico as a result of the war with Spain and would acquire the Danish West Indies in 1917, it essentially chose to create an informal, rather than a formal, empire to accomplish these goals. The Filipino people had fiercely resisted American colonial rule, and although their military resistance was eventually crushed, it soured many Americans on future colonial acquisitions, and it led to a reassertion of the old American anti-colonialism. But opposition to colonies did not mean opposition to control of an area. Indeed, opposition to colonies reinforced the desire for informal control, rather than formal control. The primary method of informal control would be the creation of five so-called "protectorates" in the area between 1901 and 1915: Cuba, Panama, Nicaragua, Haiti, and the Dominican Republic. Each of these small nations would officially remain independent but would be subject to U.S. economic and financial control, as well as U.S. military intervention under certain circumstances. Cuba was the first protectorate and, thus, the model for the protectorates that would follow.

When the United States went to war with Spain in 1898, Congress had passed the Teller Amendment, rejecting any intent to annex Cuba, and indeed, it had recognized the independence of Cuba. McKinley had agreed to this, but on his insistence, Congress had not recognized the Cuban rebels as the legitimate government of Cuba. It recognized the independence of Cuba but not the rebels as the government. McKinley, as we have seen from that famous quote to the missionaries, believed that the Cubans, as well as the Filipinos, were not yet capable of self-government. Instead, he established a U.S. military government in Cuba under General Leonard Wood, Theodore Roosevelt's friend, who had actually been the commander of the Rough Riders in Cuba.

In order to obtain an end to the U.S. military government and the withdrawal of U.S. military forces, the Cubans had to agree to the terms of the so-called Platt Amendment of 1901. This was an amendment to a U.S. Army appropriations measure. It passed the U.S. Congress. The Cubans had to then add it to their constitution, as well as agree to it in a formal treaty. By the terms of the Platt Amendment, Cuba agreed not to incur indebtedness beyond its means, something that could serve as an excuse for a European military intervention. The Cubans also agreed not to do anything else that would allow another foreign power to obtain control, and they were forced to agree to allow U.S. military intervention to enforce these terms. The Cubans further agreed, on American insistence, to a sanitation program to wipe out yellow fever. There you have the mission again.

A year after this, in 1902, a trade treaty allowed Cuban sugar into the United States at a lower U.S. tariff rate. That was a boon to the Cuban sugar industry, but it was also a move that made that sugar industry and the entire Cuban economy more dependent on the United States. U.S. troops would leave Cuba in 1902 once the Cubans had agreed to the Platt Amendment, but in 1906, President Theodore Roosevelt would order them back onto the island to end a revolution and a civil war that had broken out and to "restore order." Those troops would stay until 1909. They would return again in 1912 and then from 1917 to 1924.

Theodore Roosevelt also moved during this time to build an interoceanic canal, and that led to the creation of the Republic of Panama as a second U.S. protectorate. Panama, as previously mentioned, was a province of Colombia. It was one of the major potential routes for a canal, and it was the area in which there had been a previous—but failed—canal effort under the French engineer Ferdinand de Lesseps. The U.S. Congress had at first favored the alternative route through Nicaragua, but investors in De Lesseps's old Panama Canal Company convinced both Roosevelt and the Congress to negotiate with Colombia for the Panama route instead. A treaty was signed, but the Colombian government refused to ratify it. It demanded more money in payment for the rights to build a canal. When that happened, the investors in the Panama Canal Company organized a revolution and a new government that Theodore Roosevelt supported and quickly recognized. An ensuing treaty in 1903, the Hay-Bunau-Varilla Treaty, gave the United States the rights to a canal zone through Panama and the right to intervene militarily to protect that canal.

Roosevelt also provided the official rationale for such military interventions with his famous Roosevelt Corollary to the Monroe Doctrine. Many of these nations in the Caribbean and Central America were defaulting on their debts. European nations threatened to intervene with military force to collect those debts. Roosevelt argued that they had a right to do so, but if they did do so, they could violate the Monroe Doctrine. To prevent this from happening, Roosevelt argued in his corollary, the United States would militarily intervene for the Europeans. They would intervene militarily and financially to make sure the debts were paid. This resulted immediately in American financial supervision over the Dominican Republic, which would last until 1941. But Roosevelt's logic applied to the entire area, not just the Dominican Republic. By this corollary, as well as his specific actions, Roosevelt thus played a major role in turning the Caribbean into an American lake.

Ironically, however, a larger number of U.S. financial and military interventions would occur under Roosevelt's successors, William Howard Taft and Woodrow Wilson, than had taken place under the openly imperialistic Theodore Roosevelt. Roosevelt was proud of his imperialism and his mission concept, his civilizing mission. His two successors were not, and yet they wound up intervening more. Taft preferred loans ("dollar diplomacy") to military intervention. Stabilize these economies. Loan them the money. The borrower is the servant of the lender. But what Taft found was that such loans only led to more military interventions to protect those loans. During his one term in office, the United States would send troops back into Cuba and would establish financial supervision over Nicaragua. It would also send troops into Nicaragua from 1909 to 1910 and again in 1912. Those troops would stay until 1925 and then would come back again from 1926 to 1933.

The moralistic and supposedly anti-imperialistic Woodrow Wilson opposed both dollar diplomacy and military interventions. When he became president in 1913, he promised a major shift in Latin American policy. But as president, Wilson would send troops into the Dominican Republic and Haiti—where they would remain until 1924 and 1934, respectively—and he would send troops back into Cuba. He would also establish financial supervision over Haiti while continuing the financial supervision and military occupations that his predecessors had begun in the Dominican Republic and in Nicaragua. Wilson would also intervene massively in a revolution that erupted in Mexico during his term of office.

How does one account for this extraordinary discrepancy between Wilson's reputation and anti-imperialistic statements and the reality? One could explain it by the fact that a canal existed by now—it was finished in 1914—and a canal needed to be defended. But it was also due to the fact that Taft and Wilson shared Roosevelt's desire for control, order, and stability in the area. They were also fearful of successful European intervention in the area if instability took place and that revolutionary instability would be a signal to European powers, especially Germany, to intervene.

An additional and very important factor for Wilson was his missionary desire to spread democratic government into this area, even if it involved the use of force. This desire explains Wilson's first intervention in the Mexican Revolution of 1913–1914 in an effort to overthrow the military dictator [Victoriano] Huerta. Huerta had overthrown and murdered the constitutionalist reformer Francisco Madero, who was a hero to Wilson. He considered Huerta to be a bloody tyrant who had set back the cause of democratic reform in Mexico, and he was determined to oust him. In 1913, Wilson sent marines into Veracruz to prevent a German arms shipment from reaching Huerta. Huerta desired those arms because, even though he had murdered Madero, Madero's lieutenants— especially Venustiano Carranza and Pancho Villa, as well as Emiliano Zapata—had continued to fight on.

Wilson's intervention alienated all parties in Mexico, even though it did aid Carranza, Villa, and Zapata in overthrowing Huerta, since Huerta could not get those arms. They did overthrow him and reestablish the constitutionalist movement, but then Carranza and Villa fought for control of the country. Carranza was successful; Villa was chased up into the northern mountainous area. Defeated, Villa now turned to killing Americans. First, he stopped a train in northern Mexico, pulled Americans off the train, and shot them. He then crossed the border and attacked the town of Columbus, New Mexico.

In response, Wilson sent the United States Army into Mexico, under General John J. Pershing, with orders to capture Villa, who was labeled a bandit. Carranza had signed an agreement with Wilson allowing for hot pursuit of bandits across the border, but this turned into something far larger than hot pursuit of bandits. Villa, who knew the area like the back of his hand, sent Pershing on a wild chase, and soon Pershing's army was 300 miles deep into Mexico. We are talking about an army here of about 10,000 men. At that point, Carranza said this is intolerable [and] sent his army out with orders to surround the American army and allow it to move in only one direction, due north. Mexico and the United States were on the verge of a full-scale war.

The war was avoided. Cooler heads prevailed. Nobody really wanted war. There was a clash in which American soldiers were killed and captured, but an army investigation argued that it had been the fault of the American army captain in charge, that he had violated orders in terms of what he had done. The Mexican authorities, in turn, interpreted this as a sign of the Americans backing off, and they backed off a little bit. Each side began to back off and then, as the war in Europe continued to go on and was gradually sucking the United States in, Wilson agreed to withdraw U.S. forces.

War would, thus, be narrowly averted, and the U.S. Army would be pulled back, but this entire episode, as well as Woodrow Wilson's other behavior in Latin America, greatly expanded the informal American empire. It also provided a clear precursor to the missionary and interventionist diplomacy that Woodrow Wilson would practice in Europe during and after World War I, for World War I was occurring at the same time. Although the United States officially proclaimed its neutrality, by 1917, it would find itself deeply involved in this war. At that point, Wilson would translate his moralism and his missionary activity from Latin America to the entire world.

Lecture Twelve
"The War to End All Wars"

Scope:

In 1914, Europe erupted in general war for the first time in nearly 100 years. Despite an official declaration of neutrality, the United States declared war on Germany in April of 1917 for its violation of American neutral rights. President Woodrow Wilson insisted, however, that the United States fight the war for a far larger goal than mere defense of those rights: a new world order, based on collective security instead of the discredited balance of power, to ensure that this would be the "war to end all wars" and that the world would be made "safe for democracy." This lecture explores, first, Wilson's efforts from 1914–1917 to avoid entry into the war and why those efforts failed. We then turn to his plan to remake international relations, as enunciated in his famous "Fourteen Points" speech and other addresses. The lecture also examines the relationship between Wilson's plan and the U.S. military contribution to Allied victory in 1918.

Outline

I. In the summer of 1914, a massive war began and quickly engulfed all the major powers except the United States.

    A. On one side stood the Central Powers of Germany, Austria-Hungary, and the Ottoman Turkish Empire. On the other side were the Allied Powers of France, Russia, Great Britain, and Japan, joined in 1915 by Italy.

    B. President Woodrow Wilson quickly declared U.S. neutrality in this conflict and asked Americans to remain neutral in thought as well as action.

    C. In reality, neither Wilson, nor his advisers, nor the American people were neutral in thought or action; consequently, by 1917, the United States had entered the war on the Allied side.

II. The official reason for U.S. entry was the violation of U.S. neutral rights by German submarines, but behind this stood a host of other reasons.

A. The submarine was a new weapon of war that sank ships without warning, and its use by the Germans violated established international rules of warfare on the high seas.

B. The British navy also violated established international rules of warfare through its blockade and ship seizures.

C. The United States protested to both powers, but it held the Germans to "strict accountability" on the grounds that British violations affected American property, whereas German violations affected American lives.

   1. This position almost led to war in the spring of 1915, when a German U-boat torpedoed the British passenger liner *Lusitania*, killing 1,198 people, including 128 Americans.

   2. The crisis was temporarily resolved in the following year, when Germany, in the Arabic pledge, agreed not to sink unresisting merchant or passenger ships.

D. The Germans found Wilson's position hypocritical and had agreed to his demands only on a temporary basis. From Berlin's perspective, Wilson's "lives versus property" distinction and ensuing demands ignored numerous critical facts:

   1. The Germans suffered loss of life as a result of British violations of neutral rights.

   2. The *Lusitania* had carried munitions and was, thus, a legitimate target. The Germans had also warned Americans against travel on Allied ships.

   3. Allied merchant ships were armed and could easily destroy the fragile submarine if it surfaced and gave warning.

E. American trade with the Allies had more than tripled by 1916 and had led the Wilson administration to allow major loans to the Allies so that they could continue to purchase American war material. As a result, the United States had replaced Britain as the financial capital of the world.

F. Furthermore, Wilson and most of his key advisers were pro-Allied in their sympathies. Only Secretary of State William Jennings Bryan (1860–1925) was truly neutral, and he resigned in protest over Wilson's harsh stand in the *Lusitania* crisis.

III. Wilson did not want to enter the war and even attempted, on numerous occasions, to mediate a negotiated settlement (a "peace without victory" as he stated in early 1917). But his own blindness to the one-sidedness of his neutrality led him into a diplomatic corner from which he could not escape by April of 1917.

A. On January 31, 1917, Germany announced the resumption of unrestricted submarine warfare against all ships—neutral as well as belligerent—in a final gamble to starve Britain into submission and win the war before Germany itself collapsed from exhaustion.

B. Believing this strategy would lead to an American declaration of war, Berlin sought to keep the United States preoccupied in the Western Hemisphere through a military alliance with Mexico. Revelation of this effort with the publication of the "Zimmermann Telegram" in March 1917 infuriated previously neutral segments of the public and made Germany appear even more of a threat.

C. The overthrow of the Russian czar in the same month and the establishment of a representative government in that country made it appear that this was indeed a war of democracy versus autocracy, as British propaganda in the United States had long claimed.

D. By this time, Germany had also begun to sink U.S. merchant ships.

IV. As a result of these factors, Wilson reluctantly asked for and received from Congress, in April, a declaration of war against Germany.

A. Rather than limit his war aims to the defense of U.S. neutral rights, however, Wilson argued that the nation must fight to "make the world safe for democracy," to remake the entire international order so that another world war could never occur—a reassertion of the old American "mission" concept to remake the world in its own image.

B. To maximize his voice with the Allied powers and deal with the military crisis at hand, Wilson decided to fight the Germans on land in Europe, as well as on the high seas. The United States established a military draft, sent to Europe a large army under General John J. Pershing, and insisted that its forces remain separate from the British and French armies.

C. In his famous "Fourteen Points" speech of January 1918 and in other public statements, Wilson sketched out the essentials of his new world order, which would be based on the principles of national self-determination, democracy, and collective security instead of the failed balance of power.

D. U.S. armed forces played a major role in halting the final German offensive in the spring of 1918 and in supporting the Allied counteroffensive that led to the German request for an armistice.

E. Historians still debate whether the United States should or could have avoided entry into World War I. What is clear is that Wilson's policies did lead to U.S. entry into the war, despite his desire to avoid that outcome, and that he intended a crusade to transform the international order. The peace negotiations in Paris would determine whether or not he would succeed.

Suggested Readings:

Coogan, *The End of Neutrality.*

Gregory, *The Origins of American Intervention in the First World War.*

Link, *Woodrow Wilson.*

May, *The World War and American Isolation, 1914–1917.*

Questions to Consider:

1. Could or should the United States have avoided entry into the First World War? Why?

2. If you answered yes to the first question, what alternative policies could or should Wilson have pursued? If you answered no, do you believe Wilson's policies were appropriate and correct?

Lecture Twelve—Transcript
"The War to End All Wars"

In the summer of 1914, the archduke of the Austro-Hungarian Empire, Franz Ferdinand, was assassinated by a Serbian nationalist. This started a chain reaction that soon engulfed most of the major powers of the world in a devastating war. On one side stood the Central Powers: Germany, Austria-Hungary, and the Ottoman Turkish Empire; on the other side were the Allied Powers: France, Russia, Great Britain, Japan, and—by 1915—Italy. President Woodrow Wilson quickly declared American neutrality in this conflict, and he asked Americans to remain neutral in thought as well as action. But in reality, neither Wilson, nor his advisers, nor the American people, for that matter, were neutral in thought or in action.

For economic, cultural, and ideological reasons, a majority of the American people, as well as the president and most of his advisers, favored the Allied side—specifically, the British and the French. Britain and France were both democracies, both had deep cultural ties to the United States, and they also had deep economic ties to the United States. All of this was reinforced by British propaganda during the war, which portrayed the Germans as barbarians, especially after their 1914 invasion of neutral Belgium and reference to the treaty guaranteeing the neutrality of Belgium as "a scrap of paper." The British also maintained that the Allies were defenders of democratic values. This did present a problem since czarist Russia was on the Allied side, which British propaganda tended to ignore. The majority of Americans clearly did favor the Allied side, but favoring one side is by no means the same as being willing to fight for that side. It is easy to watch a football game on television and root for one side; it is quite a different matter to get onto the field to help that side. The same is true with a boxing match; it is one thing to root for one side in a boxing match and another thing to actually get into that fearful ring.

More important than American thoughts was the fact that American actions were not neutral. They were supposedly neutral, but in reality, they were not. Nor were they neutral in their impact on the two sides, nor in how they were viewed by the Germans. As a result, the United States would enter the war in April of 1917 on the Allied side.

A war that began in 1914 and continued into April of 1917 and beyond that into late 1918 was rather extraordinary. It was primarily the result of the unexpected military stalemate that took place on land. When the war had begun in 1914, each side had believed that it could end the war quickly and decisively through offensive action. What just about everybody missed was the fact that the new and very lethal weaponry and transportation of the Industrial Revolution had given an enormous advantage to the defense in warfare.

This had first been seen during the American Civil War, but most observers had missed it. Let me give you just one or two examples of how the defense had obtained such an advantage in war. Railroads: Theoretically, you could now run railroads right up to the front lines, deliver your troops, deliver supplies, and deliver whatever reinforcements were needed. But if you were attacking, you could not exactly build a railroad line as your troops advanced. They advanced on foot, whereas the enemy remained supplied by the railroads. The enemy also had in place heavy artillery, machine guns that would mow you down by the thousands, and a host of other weapons, all of which gave an advantage to the defense.

Consequently, with offensive operations stymied, a deadlock ensued on the western front. The soldiers began to do what they had done during the last days of the Civil War when faced with this lethal bombardment from these new tools from the Industrial Revolution: They began to dig in. Very quickly, a series of trenches was created, running all the way from the English Channel to the Swiss border. What followed were years of bloody and fruitless "trench warfare," wasting, first, thousands; then, hundreds of thousands; and eventually, millions of lives for a few hundred yards in Belgium and in northern France. In this stalemate, both sides turned to economic warfare. The British did so with their fleet via a naval blockade of Germany and its allies. The Germans turned to a new naval weapon, the submarine. This economic warfare would, in turn, eventually bring the United States into the war. The official reason for U.S. entry into the war in April of 1917 was violation of American neutral rights on the high seas by these German submarines. Behind this stood a host of other reasons that need to be delved into.

The submarine was a new weapon of war. It sank ships without warning, and in doing so, it violated the established international rules of warfare on the high seas. By those rules, established centuries earlier, a warship was required to give advance warning to unarmed enemy ships before sinking them so that passengers and crew could escape. Indeed, the warship was required to ensure the safety of those passengers and crew. The submarine did not do this. The submarine, first of all, was underwater when it attacked. It could surface, but it did not do so because the British navy was also violating established rules of international warfare, not only by its blockade of the Central Powers and its ship seizures on the high seas—actions that had led to U.S. entry into war with Britain a century earlier, in the War of 1812—but also by arming its own merchant ships, by flying the American flag or some other neutral flag on its ships. If a submarine surfaced, it was extremely fragile. It could very easily be rammed by these British merchant ships, or the deck gun on the merchant ship could sink the submarine.

The Wilson administration protested what it labeled the illegal actions of both Britain and Germany, but the protests to Germany were much more vehement. Wilson warned the Germans that they would be held to "strict accountability." His rationale for this distinction was that the British violations of neutral rights affected American property; the German violations affected American lives. This became apparent—and, indeed, it almost led to war—in 1915 when, in May of that year, a German U-boat torpedoed and sank the British passenger liner *Lusitania* off the coast of Ireland, killing 1,198 people, including 128 Americans. War fever spread.

Wilson rejected calls for war, arguing that there was such a thing as—as he put it—"too proud to fight." But in two harsh notes to Berlin, he demanded German disavowal of this act and an end to submarine warfare. The Germans proved willing only to express regret over the incident, but in the so-called *Arabic* pledge of 1915, Berlin did agree not to sink unarmed passenger ships. When the French passenger ship *Sussex* was mistakenly attacked in 1916, the Germans promised not to attack unresisting passenger or merchant ships without warning, thereby resolving the crisis, at least temporarily.

The Germans had protested. The *Lusitania*, they argued, was carrying arms and ammunition, which it was. It was, thereby, a valid target. But they were not about to go to war with the United States. They did find Wilson's position hypocritical. As we will see, they had agreed to his demands only on a temporary basis. From their perspective, Wilson's "lives versus property" distinction and his ensuing demands ignored numerous critical facts. What about the German loss of life suffered as a result of British violations of neutral rights, most notably, the illegal food blockade that Britain had instituted against Germany? What about the fact that the *Lusitania* had been carrying munitions? The Germans had also warned Americans against travel on Allied ships. Allied merchant ships, the Germans pointed out, were armed and could easily destroy the fragile submarine via deck guns or ramming if the submarine surfaced and gave warning. The submarine also was incapable of putting passengers and crew on board and taking them to safety. It simply was not big enough. It was a small, fragile craft.

Behind all these diplomatic arguments over international law, and the validity of international law, and whether it should be applied in this way at this time, in German minds also stood some very un-neutral American economic and financial ties to the Allies. American trade with the Allies had been much higher than with the Central Powers when the war started. With the Allies, it had been $825 million in 1914; with the Central Powers, only $169 million. But between 1914 and 1916, trade with the Allies exploded, jumping from $825 million to more than $3 billion. In the process, it ended an economic recession at home. At the same time, trade with the Central Powers declined to only $2 million, largely as a result of the actions of the British fleet.

This enormous expansion of trade with the Allies had led the Wilson administration to reverse its original ban on loans to the warring powers. Loans technically were allowed by international law, but Secretary of State William Jennings Bryan had argued that actually loans constituted the worst of all contraband goods. As he put it: "It commands all else." But as the trade boomed, the United States first allowed the Allies credit and then allowed outright private loans when the Allies ran out of funds so that they could continue to purchase American war material. By 1917, $2.3 billion in private loans had gone to the Allies. The trade increased further, and the total result was one of the greatest economic boom periods in U.S. history. But that also meant that the United States was economically and financially supporting the Allied war effort. In the process, the United States shifted from a debtor nation to a creditor nation. New York replaced London at this time as the financial capital of the world.

Furthermore, as previously noted, neither Wilson, nor most of his key advisers, nor the American people were neutral in thought. Almost all were pro-Allied in their sympathies, and many saw a German victory as a mortal threat to American security and to American values. Indeed, Wilson—as an academic, a political scientist writer—had virtually worshiped the British parliamentary system. His ambassador in London was vehemently pro-British. The bulk of his cabinet was pro-British. Only Secretary of State Bryan was truly neutral, and Bryan resigned in protest over Wilson's harsh stand during the *Lusitania* crisis. He would be replaced by the very pro-British Robert Lansing. With Bryan gone, his ban on loans disappeared, as well.

Similarly, Wilson used his patronage powers to squelch a congressional resolution, the so-called McLemore-Gore Resolution, which would have prohibited Americans from traveling on armed belligerent ships. Wilson insisted that the Senate and the House reject these bills, which they did on the grounds that they infringed upon American rights and his concepts of international law, which his critics labeled archaic. But this did not mean that Wilson wanted to enter the war. He did not, and he attempted on numerous occasions to have the United States mediate a negotiated settlement. In fact, he ran for reelection in 1916 on the platform that he'd kept us out of war. After his narrow reelection in 1916, he also launched a major mediation effort. On January 22, 1917, in a major public address, he openly called for a mediated "peace without victory," a negotiated settlement. But his blindness to the one-sidedness of his neutrality led him into a diplomatic corner from which he could not escape by April of 1917.

Let's go back to the Sussex pledge. The German armed forces had agreed to the Sussex pledge in 1916 only because they did not have enough submarines to achieve decisive victory. They thus agreed with the civilian leadership not to push the United States into the war at that time. Indeed, in retrospect, what may be truly extraordinary is how few of these underwater craft were actually involved in this entire crisis. The entire German submarine fleet in 1914 consisted of only 21 vessels. At their peak in October of 1917, there were only 127 such vessels, of which only one-third operated at any time, but there was no defense against them. By January of 1917, the German armed forces concluded that the number that they had was sufficient to make a difference—and quickly.

On January 31, 1917, only a little over a week since Wilson's peace without victory address, Germany thus reversed policy and announced the resumption of unrestricted submarine warfare—now against all ships, unarmed as well as armed, neutral as well as belligerent—in a final gamble to starve Britain into submission and win the war before Germany itself collapsed from the sheer exhaustion of the years of fighting. From Berlin's perspective, the United States was already a belligerent from an economic and a financial point of view, and the Germans gambled that they could starve Britain out in five months and end the war before the United States could mobilize and send any soldiers to Europe. Four days after the German declaration of unrestricted submarine warfare, Wilson severed diplomatic relations with Berlin, but that did not mean war. He still tried to avoid entering the war during February and March of 1917; that effort failed.

Berlin believed that its declaration of unrestricted submarine warfare would lead to an American declaration of war, and as a result, it secretly sought to keep the United States preoccupied in the Western Hemisphere. The best way to do that was a military alliance with Mexico, with [which] Wilson—as we saw in the last lecture—had almost gone to war in 1916. The German foreign minister, Arthur Zimmermann, thus asked the German ambassador in Mexico to sound out Carranza on a possible military alliance against the United States and, in the event of war, to offer help in reconquering the territories Mexico had lost to the United States in the 1830s and the 1840s: Texas, California, and New Mexico. Zimmermann also proposed getting Japan to change sides in the war as a means of keeping the United States preoccupied in the Pacific, as well as the Western Hemisphere, and thus, out of Europe. But British intelligence intercepted this so-called "Zimmermann Telegram" and handed it over to Wilson, who released it to the press on March 1, 1917. Wilson had also asked Congress for the authority to arm U.S. merchant ships by this time. The telegram infuriated previously neutral segments of the public and made Germany appear even more of a threat than it had merely by the declaration of unrestricted submarine warfare.

Then, in mid-March, the Russian czar was overthrown. He was forced to abdicate, and a provisional representative government was established in Russia. That made it appear that this was, indeed, a war of democracy on one side against autocracy on the other, as

British propaganda in the United States had long argued. By this time, Wilson had, on his own executive authority, ordered the arming of U.S. merchant ships. He did so because of a filibuster in the Senate [conducted by] dissidents that Wilson referred to as a "band of willful men." At the same time, Germany began to sink U.S. merchant ships.

Still, Wilson held back. "Once lead this people into war," he supposedly warned, "and they will forget what a thing tolerance is"—something that proved quite true. He was also afraid that by entering the war, the United States would be so preoccupied in Europe that what he referred to as the "yellow peril," Japan, would be able to run amok in the Pacific. But the pressure for war was now simply overwhelming. As a result of all of these factors, Wilson reluctantly asked for and received from Congress in April a declaration of war against Germany. It was not a unanimous vote—far from it: 373 to 50 in the House of Representatives and 82 to 6 in the Senate—but clearly, the war vote passed by large majorities.

Rather than limit his war aims to a defense of U.S. neutral rights, however, Wilson argued in his war message to Congress that the nation must fight to "make the world safe for democracy." What he called for was a war to remake the entire international order so that another world war could never take place. In doing this, Wilson was, in effect, reasserting and expanding the old American "mission" concept, which we have referred to again and again in this course. He was reasserting it, and expanding it, and saying that the United States was, indeed, now going to remake the world in its own image—this time via the sword.

To maximize his voice vis-à-vis the leaders of the Allied Powers who might not support this program and to deal with the military crisis at hand—and the Allies were facing a military crisis at this time—Wilson decided to fight the Germans on land in Europe, as well as on the high seas. Stop and think about this for a minute. If you're going to war because of the German declaration of unrestricted submarine warfare, theoretically, you could have gotten away with simply a naval war, as you had had against France in 1798–1799. But Wilson decides, no, the United States will fight on land, as well. There is a military crisis, but also this will strengthen his hand at the peace conference. Consequently, the United States establishes a military draft and sends a large army to Europe, the

American Expeditionary Forces under General John J. Pershing. Both Pershing and Wilson insist that this force remain separate from the British and French armies. The British and French wish to amalgamate American units into their armies. Wilson and Pershing said no, the American army is to remain separate.

U.S. forces would play a major role in halting the final German land offensive in the spring of 1918. They would also play a major role in the ensuing Allied counteroffensive in the fall of 1918, most notably, at St. Mihiel and in the Meuse-Argonne. The success of this offensive, this Allied offensive, all along the line in the fall of 1918, after their own offensive had been halted during the summer, led the German military to request an armistice. The Allies agreed but on terms that made clear that Germany could not resume hostilities again. On the 11th hour of the 11th day of the 11th month of 1918, an armistice went into effect—which, in effect, halted one of the bloodiest wars in human history. By that time, Germany's allies had already surrendered, and U.S. forces occupied approximately 23 percent of the Allied line. Clearly, those forces had played a major role in Allied military successes, and Wilson would play a major role in the ensuing peace conference.

In January of 1918, Wilson had outlined his peace program in his famous "Fourteen Points" speech. He had amplified upon this in other public statements in 1918. What Wilson wanted to do was nothing less than [to] create a new world order to replace the old system of European power politics that he argued had led to this war, as well as countless previous wars. Secret treaties and secret diplomacy would be replaced by "open covenants, ... openly arrived at." Those open covenants would secure freedom of the seas [and] the removal of tariff barriers, would establish equal trade opportunities, and would lead to a dramatic reduction in armaments to a level needed only for "domestic safety." Furthermore, nations occupied during the war were to be evacuated and restored to sovereignty, while the old multinational empires run by kings and emperors were to be destroyed and replaced by national self-determination for their minority groups and democratically elected governments, with appropriate territorial adjustments.

Furthermore, the balance-of-power system that had failed to keep the peace in 1914 would now be replaced by what Wilson referred to as "a general association of nations" that would guarantee the political independence and territorial integrity of all via the principle of "collective security"—that is, the establishment of an international body and legal system whereby all nations would agree to resolve their disputes peacefully and to act in unison against any aggressor nation. Collective security was to be the wave of the future; the balance of power had failed and would be rejected.

Historians still debate whether the United States should or could have avoided entry into the First World War. Would a German victory have threatened the security of the nation? Did such thoughts of security even enter Woodrow Wilson's calculations? Were there alternative policies that should have been pursued? Historians still argue over all of these questions. What is clear is that Wilson's policies did lead to American entry into the war, despite his desire not to do so, and that he decided to join the war as a crusade to remake the entire international order. The ensuing peace negotiations in Paris, which Wilson would attend personally, would determine whether or not he would succeed. It is to those negotiations in Paris that we must now turn.

Timeline

1823	Monroe Doctrine.
1830	Indian Removal Act.
1835–1836	Texan revolution.
1842	Webster-Ashburton Treaty; Tyler Doctrine extends Monroe Doctrine to Hawaii.
1844	Treaty of Wangxia with China.
1845	Annexation of Texas.
1846	War with Mexico begins; Oregon settlement with Britain.
1848	Acquisition of California and New Mexico via the Treaty of Guadalupe Hidalgo.
1853–1854	Perry mission and Treaty of Kanagawa with Japan.
1861–1865	American Civil War.
1866	Maximilian affair comes to a head in Mexico.
1867	Purchase of Alaska.
1871	Treaty of Washington with Britain.
1890	Bureau of Census declares the end of the frontier; Mahan's *Influence of Sea Power upon History* published.
1893	Hawaiian revolution; depression of 1893.
1895	Venezuelan crisis and Olney Corollary to the Monroe Doctrine.
1898–1899	War with Spain and acquisition of Puerto Rico, Hawaii, Guam, the Philippines, and Samoa.
1899–1900	Open Door Notes.
1901	Platt Amendment for Cuba.

1903	Panamanian revolution and Panama Canal Treaty.
1904–1905	Roosevelt Corollary to the Monroe Doctrine.
1913–1916	Military interventions in Mexican revolution.
1914	World War I begins.
1915	*Lusitania* crisis.
1917	U.S. entry into World War I.
1918–1920	End of World War I; Paris Peace Conference; Senate rejection of the Treaty of Versailles and the League of Nations Covenant.
1921–1922	Washington Naval Conference and Four-, Five-, and Nine-Power Treaties.
1924–1925	Dawes Plan and Locarno Treaties.
1928	Kellogg-Briand Pact.
1930	London Naval Conference and Treaty.
1931–1932	Japanese seizure of Manchuria and creation of Manchukuo.
1933	Japan quits the League of Nations; Hitler takes power in Germany; United States officially recognizes the U.S.S.R.
1935–1939	Axis aggression in Asia and Europe; U.S. Neutrality Acts; World War II begins in Europe.
1940	Germany conquers Western Europe; Axis Tripartite Pact.

1941 ....Lend-Lease Act; Germany invades
U.S.S.R.; Atlantic Charter;
undeclared naval war in the
Atlantic; Pearl Harbor attacked;
United States enters World War II.

1942–1943 ....Declaration by United Nations;
second front controversy;
unconditional surrender policy
developed; Tehran Conference.

1945 ....Yalta Conference; death of FDR;
German surrender; Potsdam
Conference; atom bomb attacks on
Hiroshima and Nagasaki;
Japanese surrender.

1946 ....Kennan's "Long Telegram";
Churchill's "Iron Curtain" speech.

1947 ....Truman Doctrine; Marshall Plan;
containment policy developed.

1948–1949 ....Berlin blockade; formation of West
Germany and NATO; Soviet Union
tests its first nuclear weapon;
Communist victory in China.

1950–1951 ....NSC-68; Korean War begins;
Truman-MacArthur controversy.

1953–1954 ....CIA overthrow of Mosaddeq in Iran
and Arbenz in Guatemala; Geneva
Conference on Indochina; formation
of SEATO.

1955 ....Diem takes power in
South Vietnam.

1956 ....Suez crisis.

1957–1959 ....Eisenhower Doctrine; Lebanon
intervention; Castro takes power in
Cuba; U-2 Affair.

1961 ....Bay of Pigs invasion; Berlin
Wall constructed.

1962	Cuban Missile Crisis.
1963	Nuclear Test-Ban Treaty; Diem and Kennedy assassinations.
1964	Tonkin Gulf episode and resolution.
1965	Major expansion of U.S. military commitment in Vietnam; military intervention in the Dominican Republic.
1966	Fulbright hearings begin.
1967	Arab-Israeli Six-Day War.
1968	Tet Offensive; Johnson's call for peace talks and announcement that he will not seek reelection.
1969	Nixon Doctrine.
1972	Nixon visits to China and Moscow; SALT I; Berlin/German Accords.
1973	Paris Peace Accords on Vietnam; overthrow of Allende in Chile; Yom Kippur War and oil crisis.
1974	Watergate crisis and Nixon resignation; Vladivostok summit.
1975	Helsinki Accords; Communist victory in Vietnam.
1977	Panama Canal Treaties.
1978–1979	Camp David Accords and Egypt-Israel peace treaty; Iranian Revolution and hostage crisis; second oil shock; Soviet invasion of Afghanistan.
1980	Carter Doctrine.

1981–1985....................................Reagan Doctrine; military buildup and interventions in Central America, the Caribbean, and the Middle East; new Soviet-American conflicts.

1985–1988....................................Gorbachev takes power in the U.S.S.R. and announces *glasnost* and *perestroika*; Geneva, Iceland, and Moscow summits; INF Treaty.

1989–1991....................................End of the Soviet Empire in Eastern Europe; START I; Panama invasion; German reunification; Soviet Union collapses; first Iraq war.

Glossary

agrarianism: According to this philosophy, American liberty and representative government are best maintained by a rural society of independent small farmers. This belief is usually associated with Thomas Jefferson and his followers and played a major role in American territorial expansion.

balance of power: A method of preserving peace by having nations so balanced against each other that each is afraid to start a war for fear of losing. The numerous failures of this approach, especially in 1914, led to support for collective security as an alternative approach.

Bolshevism: This radical Marxist ideology, which called for the violent overthrow of all capitalist governments, triumphed in Russia during World War I and resulted in the creation of the Soviet Union.

brinksmanship: A term used to describe and criticize the aggressive anti-Soviet foreign policy and "massive retaliation" defense policy based on nuclear weapons during the Eisenhower presidency. This combination meant that numerous Cold War crises during these years would go to the brink of nuclear war.

"cash and carry": In an effort to avoid entry into another war, Congress, in the Neutrality Acts of the 1930s, banned U.S. ships from carrying goods and U.S. citizens from providing loans to belligerent powers. Those powers could purchase U.S. goods only if they paid for them directly and carried them away in their own ships.

collective security: As championed by Woodrow Wilson and embedded in the League of Nations Covenant, as well as the later U.N. Charter, this concept sought to replace the balance of power as a peacekeeping device with a legal framework for collective international action against any aggressor nation.

containment: The U.S. policy to contain Soviet and communist expansion throughout the Cold War. Authored by George F. Kennan in 1947, the policy took different forms in different administrations, many of which Kennan himself opposed.

continentalism: The early and mid-19th-century U.S. policy to expand across the entire North American continent.

contraband: Technically defined as anything prohibited by law from being imported or exported, this term usually refers to instruments of war that are liable, according to international law, to seizure by belligerent powers from neutral ships. The United States tended to define contraband in narrow terms (i.e., guns and munitions), whereas the British defined contraband in much broader terms (food and clothing), leading to numerous conflicts between the two nations during the years 1793–1812 and 1914–1917, as well as a war in 1812.

détente: A lessening of tensions between belligerent powers that was used (and misunderstood by many) to explain Soviet-American relations in the Nixon-Ford-Kissinger era.

doctrine of the two spheres: A belief that the Eastern and Western hemispheres constituted two distinct geographic units and that states of war and peace did not necessarily apply to both spheres at the same time.

"dollar diplomacy": A term usually associated with President William Howard Taft but also used by his successors and his predecessor, Theodore Roosevelt. This policy sought to use American financial and economic power to obtain desired political results in other nations. It was first used in Central America and the Caribbean.

entente: Informal understanding between two or more nations.

"Europe first": The global strategy of the United States and its World War II allies to concentrate on the defeat of Germany before Japan and, therefore, on offensive operations in the European theater, while maintaining the strategic defensive in Asia and the Pacific. It was the basic U.S. and Allied strategy during the war but was violated in practice. The doctrinal primacy of Europe over Asia continued during the Cold War, as did the violations in practice.

fascism: A highly militaristic 20th-century ideology that triumphed in Germany, Italy, Japan, and numerous other countries; fascism is considered a major cause of the Second World War.

Federalism: A division of power between the state and national governments instituted under the new Constitution in 1789.

"flexible response": The new U.S. defense policy instituted in the Kennedy administration that rejected Eisenhower's reliance primarily on nuclear weapons and focused on a buildup of conventional and counterinsurgency forces.

"free ships make free goods": This U.S. position on neutral rights maintained that a neutral ship could carry non-contraband goods of a belligerent power without being subject to seizure.

free trade: A strong belief throughout U.S. history that trade should be conducted without tariff barriers and that it could serve as an alternative to war.

idealism: A belief that international relations can and should be conducted on the basis of moral and legal principles instead of raw power.

impressment: The practice of forcibly drafting individuals into military service. Practiced extensively by the British navy during the late 18th and early 19th centuries, the resulting seizure of sailors from U.S. ships was a major cause of the War of 1812.

"informal empire": This domination of one nation or people over another without the formal acquisition of colonies was a hallmark of U.S. foreign policy after the Spanish-American War.

isolationism: Although this term has traditionally been used to describe American policy before World War II vis-à-vis the rest of the world, numerous historians have challenged its validity save in regard to formal alliances with European powers.

League of Nations: The international body based on the principle of collective security that was championed by Woodrow Wilson and created in the Treaty of Versailles but rejected by the U.S. Senate in 1919–1920.

lend-lease: The U.S. policy from early 1941 through 1945 to provide, first, Britain, then the Soviet Union and other nations fighting the Axis Powers with war material free of charge.

Manifest Destiny: A term coined by New York newspaper editor John O'Sullivan in 1839, Manifest Destiny refers to the belief that the United States is a special, covenanted nation, destined by God's will to expand over the entire North American continent and become the greatest country in human history.

Marshall Plan: Officially labeled the European Recovery Program, this major and highly successful U.S. policy during the early years of the Cold War provided West European nations with massive aid to rebuild their war-shattered economies in an integrated manner.

"massive retaliation": A popular description of the defense policy of the Eisenhower administration that, rejecting the deficit spending of its predecessor, relied upon relatively inexpensive nuclear weapons over conventional forces.

mission concept: This belief in a unique American mission to remake the world in its own image has been a strong component of U.S. foreign policies since the colonial era, though Americans have often disagreed sharply about whether it should be done by force or by example.

Monroe Doctrine: Delivered as part of the president's annual message to Congress in December of 1823, this famous document asserted that the Western and Eastern hemispheres constituted two distinct political systems, as well as distinct geographical entities, and that the former was no longer open to European colonization or intervention. It was largely the work of John Quincy Adams, resulting from an earlier British offer for a joint statement and, for many years, was enforced by the British fleet. Later corollaries made it a tool for American domination of the Western Hemisphere.

most favored nation: A clause in many U.S. trade treaties whereby any future benefits in tariff rates granted by either signatory to a third party would automatically accrue to the other signatory.

no transfer: A principle usually associated with the Monroe Doctrine but actually asserted both before and after. This U.S. policy opposed the transfer of any colony in the Western Hemisphere from one European power to another.

NSC-68: An early-1950 National Security Council Paper that called for a new defense policy based on a major military buildup of the United States and its allies, no matter what the financial cost, in order to counter what was labeled a global and monolithic communist threat. Written primarily by Paul Nitze in the aftermath of Soviet detonation of an atomic device, it became a reality as a result of the Korean War.

Open Door: Formally enunciated in the Open Door Notes of 1899 and 1900, this U.S. policy called for equal trade opportunities in China, along with preservation of the territorial and administrative integrity of that nation.

perestroika and *glasnost*: This attempted restructuring and liberalization of the Soviet economic and political systems by Mikhail Gorbachev during the 1980s was a major factor in the warming of Soviet-American relations and the ensuing end to the Cold War.

protectorate: A term used to describe a nominally independent nation that is actually controlled by another power. The United States had five protectorates in Central America and the Caribbean as part of the informal empire it created in the early 20th century.

rapprochement: A warming of relations between powers that goes beyond the lessening of tensions involved in détente.

realism: A belief that international relations are and will continue to be based on considerations of power rather than legal and moral principles.

republicanism: This belief in representative government was the central ideology in the formation of the United States, and a desire to spread it to other nations has long been a key component of U.S. foreign policy.

right of deposit: The right to deposit produce brought down the Mississippi River at Spanish-controlled New Orleans so that it could be reloaded onto oceangoing vessels. This right, critical to western farmers, was obtained in Pinckney's Treaty of 1795 and threatened by Spain's cession of Louisiana to France in 1800.

Romanticism: This early 19th-century worldview replaced the rationalism and universalism of the 18th-century Enlightenment with an emphasis on emotion and particularism. It played a major role in the ensuing development of "scientific" racism and other key components of 19th-century American expansionism.

"scientific" racism: This 19th- and early 20th-century belief in the inherent superiority and inferiority of specific races based on pseudo-scientific "evidence" played a major role in the dispossession and forced removal of Native American tribes; the acquisition of Texas, California, and New Mexico from Mexico via war; and the southern defense of slavery before the Civil War. It played an equally important role in the later segregation and disenfranchisement of blacks, U.S. immigration restrictions, and the genocidal policies of Nazi Germany.

Second Great Awakening: This major evangelical religious revival in the early 19th century had a profound impact on numerous aspects of American life, including foreign policy. Its belief in universal salvation, societal perfectibility, and the United States as God's chosen nation fueled an aggressive territorial expansion, along with overseas expansion via missionary activity in Asia and the Pacific.

second-front controversy: This major conflict in the World War II grand alliance over how to defeat Nazi Germany pitted the British peripheral approach in the Mediterranean against Soviet and American insistence on cross-channel operations. It resulted in the Anglo-American invasions of North Africa, Sicily, and Italy in 1942–1943; the ensuing delay of cross-channel operations until 1944; and much bitterness within the alliance.

Truman Doctrine: In a 1947 request to Congress for aid to the Greek government in its struggle against Communist guerrillas and a Turkish government facing Soviet pressure, President Truman asserted this key Cold War policy of supporting "free peoples" who were "resisting attempted subjugation by armed minorities or by outside pressures."

unilateralism: Seen by many historians as a more accurate description than isolationism of traditional U.S. policy toward other nations, unilateralism describes an American desire and tendency to act on its own in the world, without the encumbrances of alliances.

United Nations: This international body, based on the principle of collective security, was created at the end of World War II to replace the League of Nations.

Wilsonianism: A term referring to the foreign policies of Woodrow Wilson that is often used to describe U.S. efforts to promote collective security, to spread democracy to other nations, or to re-create the world in the American image.

Biographical Notes

Acheson, Dean (1893–1971): Undersecretary of state and secretary of state during the Truman administration. He was important in the creation and implementation of major U.S. policies during the early years of the Cold War and the Korean conflict and was a primary target of Republicans for his haughtiness, as well as his policies.

Adams, John (1735–1826): As second president of the United States, Adams's willingness to end the undeclared naval war with France was an extraordinary act of political courage that may have saved the nation from civil war but split his Federalist Party and led to his defeat for reelection in 1800.

Adams, John Quincy (1767–1848): Considered by many historians to have been America's greatest secretary of state, Adams's accomplishments included engineering the rapprochement with Great Britain that followed the War of 1812, acquiring Florida from Spain, securing a U.S. claim to Oregon, and authoring the Monroe Doctrine.

Bryan, William Jennings (1860–1925): In addition to his three unsuccessful presidential bids, this major political figure served as Woodrow Wilson's secretary of state from 1913–1915. He disagreed with Wilson's neutrality policies, resigned in protest, and was replaced by Robert Lansing.

Dulles, John Foster (1888–1959): Secretary of state under Eisenhower who appeared to be running U.S. foreign policy and whose excessive moralism and ideological rigidity alienated many.

Fulbright, J. William (1905–1995): As chair of the Senate Foreign Relations Committee during the 1960s, Fulbright became a major critic of the Vietnam War and what he labeled America's "arrogance of power."

Hamilton, Alexander (1755–1804): The first secretary of the treasury and a major adviser to George Washington, Hamilton played a pivotal role in the creation and implementation of a pro-British foreign policy, as well as U.S. fiscal and military policies during the 1790s.

Hay, John (1838–1905): Secretary of state who issued the famous Open Door Notes in 1899 and 1900, asserting U.S. support for equal trade opportunities in China and the preservation of that country's territorial and administrative integrity.

Hoover, Herbert (1874–1964): Before his failed presidency of 1929–1933, Hoover played a major role as secretary of commerce from 1921–1928 in the expansion of American trade and influence that undergirded the prosperity and peace of the 1920s.

Hughes, Charles Evans (1862–1948): Narrowly defeated by Woodrow Wilson in the 1916 presidential campaign, Hughes became secretary of state during the ensuing Harding administration and was primarily responsible for the successful naval arms limitation conference in Washington that resulted in the Four-, Five-, and Nine-Power Treaties and helped to ensure a decade of peace in Asia and the Pacific.

Jay, John (1745–1829): A major diplomatic figure in early American history, as well as one of the three authors of the famous Federalist papers and chief justice of the Supreme Court. He served as a representative to Spain and a peace negotiator during the Revolutionary War, secretary of foreign affairs under the Articles of Confederation, and negotiator of the 1794 treaty with Britain that bears his name.

Jefferson, Thomas (1743–1826): Although he is best known as the author of the Declaration of Independence and third president of the United States, Jefferson was also the nation's first secretary of state and the key opponent of Hamilton's foreign and domestic policies. As president, his Louisiana Purchase more than doubled the size of the United States.

Kennan, George F. (1904–2005): A career foreign service officer and Russian specialist who headed the State Department's Policy Planning staff from 1947–1950 and served as ambassador to the U.S.S.R. and Yugoslavia. Kennan authored the famous "Long Telegram" and containment policy vis-à-vis the Soviet Union before becoming a scholar and major critic of the Cold War policies he had helped to initiate.

Kissinger, Henry A. (b. 1923): A Harvard political scientist who became national security adviser and secretary of state during the Nixon-Ford presidencies, Kissinger played a key role in the major reorientation of U.S. foreign policy that occurred from 1969–1976. He is generally considered one of the most important and controversial figures in the history of American foreign policy.

Lodge, Henry Cabot (1850–1924): Republican senator from Massachusetts and friend of Theodore Roosevelt who strongly supported U.S. overseas imperialism during the late 19th and early 20th centuries. As chair of the Senate Foreign Relations Committee, he led the successful fight against Senate ratification of Woodrow Wilson's Treaty of Versailles and League of Nations Covenant.

Madison, James (1751–1836): Although far less famous than his colleague Jefferson, Madison is considered the father of the Constitution and co-founder of the Democratic-Republican Party that opposed Hamilton's policies. He served as secretary of state under Jefferson from 1801–1809 and as president from 1809–1817.

Mahan, Alfred Thayer (1840–1914): Probably the most famous naval theoretician of all time, Mahan, in his prominent 1890 work, *Influence of Sea Power upon History*, and other writings, argued that the oceans were highways rather than defensive moats and that sea power was the key to national greatness. His ideas played a major role in the creation of the modern U.S. Navy, the acquisition of a colonial empire in the Caribbean and Pacific, and the building of a canal through Central America.

Marshall, George C. (1880–1959): One of the most important and respected individuals in the 1940s, Marshall served as army chief of staff from 1939–1945, special presidential envoy to China immediately thereafter, secretary of state from 1947–1949, and secretary of defense from 1950–1951. In these roles, he was a major figure in the creation of America's awesome military power and Allied victory during World War II and the development and success of early U.S. Cold War policies, most notably, the Marshall Plan for European economic recovery that bears his name and for which he won the Nobel Peace Prize.

McNamara, Robert (b. 1916): Controversial secretary of defense under Kennedy and Johnson from 1963–1967, McNamara was one of the chief architects of U.S. national security policies during his tenure and supported the major military commitment to Vietnam that occurred during those years.

Olney, Richard (1835–1917): Secretary of state during the Venezuelan crisis of 1895 and author of the famous Olney Corollary to the Monroe Doctrine, asserting a U.S. right to arbitrate disputes between European and Latin American nations.

O'Sullivan, John (1813–1895): New York newspaper editor who coined the phrase "Manifest Destiny" in 1839.

Polk, James K. (1795–1849): As president from 1845–1849, Polk was responsible for the acquisition of Oregon peacefully and of California and New Mexico through war. Polk is one of the least known but most important presidents in the history of American continental expansion. He is also one of the most controversial, rated as near great by some historians but attacked by others for initiating an unnecessary war of aggression that led directly to the Civil War and for a dangerous expansion of presidential war-making powers.

Seward, William Henry (1801–1872): A former New York governor and senator, Seward served as secretary of state from 1861–1869. He is best known for his diplomacy during the Civil War, which succeeded in preventing European intervention on the side of the South, but he is equally important for his postwar acquisition of Alaska from Russia and for his expansionist vision of a global American empire.

Tecumseh (1768–1813): Shawnee diplomat and warrior who created and led a major confederation of Native American tribes along the frontier in an effort to halt further white expansion in the early 19th century. The effort at first succeeded but eventually led to the War of 1812, during which Tecumseh was killed.

Tracy, Benjamin F. (1830–1915): Secretary of the navy in the Harrison presidency of 1889–1893, Tracy is considered the father of the modern U.S. Navy.

Trist, Nicholas P. (1800–1874): Chief clerk of the State Department who violated presidential orders in 1847–1848 to negotiate the Treaty of Guadalupe Hidalgo that ended the war with Mexico and gained California and New Mexico for the United States.

Turner, Frederick Jackson (1861–1932): Famous U.S. historian whose "frontier thesis" of 1893 is often viewed as a key primary source for understanding U.S. overseas imperialism and a major secondary interpretation of American history.

Tyler, John (1790–1862): The first vice president to assume the presidency upon the death of an incumbent (in this case, William Henry Harrison), Tyler extended the Monroe Doctrine to Hawaii and pressed for the annexation of the Republic of Texas. He achieved this goal just a few days before he left office through a joint resolution that required only majority votes instead of a treaty that would have required a two-thirds Senate vote.

Walker, William (1824–1860): Known as the "grey-eyed man of destiny," Walker was one of the most famous filibusters—individuals who forcibly attempted to create personal empires in Central America and the Caribbean during the time between the war with Mexico and the Civil War. At one point, Walker succeeded in gaining control over Nicaragua and recognition from Washington, but he was eventually overthrown and killed.

Webster, Daniel (1782–1852): Famous Massachusetts congressman and senator who served as secretary of state from 1841–1843 and again from 1850–1852. On both occasions, he played a major role in American commercial expansion into the Pacific and Far East.

Bibliography

Allison, Graham T., and Philip D. Zelikow. *Essence of Decision: Explaining the Cuban Missile Crisis.* 2nd ed. New York: Longman, 1999. First published in 1971, this path-breaking study in political science explored multiple alternative approaches to the crisis, as well as the standard "rational actor" model.

Beisner, Robert L., ed. *American Foreign Relations Since 1600: A Guide to the Literature.* 2nd ed. 2 vols. Santa Barbara, CA: ABC-CLIO, 2003. Sponsored by the Society for Historians of American Foreign Relations, this invaluable guide provides annotated bibliographical citations for more than 16,000 works in the field.

———. *From the Old Diplomacy to the New, 1865–1900.* 2nd ed. Arlington Heights, IL: Harlan Davidson, 1986. This brief volume offers an excellent introduction to the rise of America as an imperial power after the Civil War. It covers the numerous interpretive disputes surrounding that rise, the actual events, and the author's own interpretation of a paradigm shift during these years in the views and behavior of American policymakers.

Bemis, Samuel Flagg. *John Quincy Adams and the Foundations of American Foreign Policy.* New York: Alfred A. Knopf, 1949 (Norton 1973 reprint). This classic work helped to establish Adams's reputation as one of the foremost American secretaries of state.

Beschloss, Michael. *The Crisis Years: Kennedy and Krushchev, 1960–1963.* New York: Edward Burlingame Books, 1991. A lengthy, bestselling analysis of the numerous Cold War crises that occurred during these years, with an emphasis on the two leaders.

Borg, Dorothy, and Waldo H. Heinrichs, eds. *Uncertain Years: Chinese-American Relations.* New York: Columbia University Press, 1980. This collection contains many useful and important essays on Sino-American relations from the end of World War II to the outbreak of the Korean War.

Braeman, John. "Power and Diplomacy: The 1920s Reappraised." *Review of Politics* 44 (July 1982): 342–369. This important article argues that U.S. policies from 1921–1933 were not naïve or unwise and that the nation enjoyed unmatched security during this period.

Brown, Roger H. *The Republic in Peril: 1812.* New York: Columbia University Press, 1964 (Norton 1971 reprint). This detailed and important analysis of the vote for war in 1812 emphasizes partisan as opposed to sectional considerations.

Campbell, Charles S. *The Transformation of American Foreign Relations, 1865–1900.* New York: Harper and Row, 1976. This comprehensive survey focuses on the transformation of the U.S. position in the world in the years after the Civil War, with an emphasis on changes in relations with Great Britain.

Carroll, John M., and George C. Herring, eds. *Modern American Diplomacy.* 2nd ed. Wilmington, DE: Scholarly Resources, 1996. A collection of useful introductory essays on key events and issues in 20th-century U.S. foreign policy.

Cohen, Warren, ed. *The Cambridge History of American Foreign Relations.* 4 vols. New York: Cambridge University Press, 1993. Each of the volumes in this chronological series was written by a distinguished diplomatic historian (Bradford Perkins for 1776–1865, Walter LaFeber for 1865–1913, Akira Iriye for 1913–1945, and Warren Cohen for 1945–1991). Each volume also has a different title and contains a different interpretation for the years under study.

————. *Empire without Tears: America's Foreign Relations, 1921–1933.* Philadelphia, PA: Temple University Press, 1987. A brief and useful analysis of Republican and business efforts to create a stable world order during this era.

Collin, Richard H. *Theodore Roosevelt's Caribbean: The Panama Canal, the Monroe Doctrine, and the Latin American Context.* Baton Rouge, LA: Louisiana State University Press, 1990. The author emphasizes Roosevelt's fear of European aggression as a motivating factor in explaining and defending his behavior in the area.

Combs, Jerald. *American Diplomatic History: Two Centuries of Conflicting Interpretations.* Berkeley, CA: University of California Press, 1983. A major historiographic analysis of conflicting interpretations of U.S. foreign policy from the Revolution to the early 1980s. For historiographical analyses of specific episodes and time periods, see Michael J. Hogan's two edited collections, *America in the World* (post-1941) and *Paths to Power* (pre-1941) (New York: Cambridge University Press, 1995 and 2000).

————. *The Jay Treaty: Political Battleground of the Founding Fathers.* Berkeley, CA: University of California Press, 1970. A detailed and important analysis of the numerous factors that lay behind the partisan split over this treaty.

Coogan, John W. *The End of Neutrality: The United States, Britain, and Maritime Rights, 1899–1915*. Ithaca, NY: Cornell University Press, 1981. An analysis of prewar and wartime Anglo-American negotiations over neutral rights that criticizes Wilson's position on those rights as heavily pro-Allied.

Cooper, John Milton. *Breaking the Heart of the World: Woodrow Wilson and the Fight for the League of Nations*. New York: Cambridge University Press, 2001. This is the most recent and detailed treatment of the Senate defeat of the League.

Costigliola, Frank C. *Awkward Dominion: American Political, Economic, and Cultural Relations with Europe, 1919–1933*. Ithaca, NY: Cornell University Press, 1984. An analysis that emphasizes American unofficial diplomacy and cultural expansion during this era.

Crook, D. P. *The North, the South, and the Powers, 1861–1865*. New York: Wiley, 1974. This comprehensive history analyzes American issues during the Civil War in the context of worldwide diplomacy. An abridged edition was published in 1975 as *Diplomacy during the American Civil War*.

Dallek, Robert. *Franklin D. Roosevelt and American Foreign Policy, 1932–1945*. New York: Oxford University Press, 1979. The most comprehensive and extensive study of Roosevelt's foreign policies during his presidency, this volume largely defends FDR against his critics and emphasizes both his accomplishments and the constraints under which he had to work.

Dangerfield, George. *The Era of Good Feelings*. New York: Harcourt, Brace, 1952. This prize-winning history offers excellent and highly readable detail on U.S. foreign relations and domestic issues from the War of 1812 to 1828, with an emphasis on John Quincy Adams and Anglo-American relations.

DeConde, Alexander. *Entangling Alliance: Politics and Diplomacy under George Washington*. Durham, NC: Duke University Press, 1958. This volume focuses on Alexander Hamilton and the relationship between domestic politics and diplomacy during the Washington administration.

———. *The Quasi War: The Politics and Diplomacy of the Undeclared War with France, 1797–1801*. New York: Scribner, 1966. A detailed study of the origins, course, and consequences of this relatively ignored but very important war in U.S. history.

————. *This Affair of Louisiana*. New York: Scribner, 1976. This full-length history of the Louisiana Purchase emphasizes the drive for Louisiana as part of an aggressive expansionist tradition, with Jefferson playing an important, activist role.

DeConde, Alexander, Richard Dean Burns, and Fred Logevall, eds. *Encyclopedia of American Foreign Policy: Studies of the Principal Movements and Ideas*. Rev. ed., 3 vols. New York: Charles Scribner's Sons, 2003. A collection of scholarly essays and brief bibliographies by distinguished specialists of broad concepts in the field.

Divine, Robert A. *Eisenhower and the Cold War*. New York: Oxford University Press, 1981. A brief and early revisionist account that praises Eisenhower for his restraint and sound judgment.

Doenecke, Justus D., and John E. Wilz, *From Isolation to War, 1931–1941*. 3rd ed. Arlington Heights, IL: Harlan Davidson, 2003. A combined narrative and historiographical essay that covers the events and interpretive disputes regarding the coming of World War II and U.S. entry into the war.

Dull, Jonathan R. *A Diplomatic History of the American Revolution*. New Haven, CT: Yale University Press, 1985. An excellent, up-to-date analysis of the diplomacy of the American Revolution.

Edmonds, Robin. *The Big Three: Churchill, Roosevelt, and Stalin in Peace and War*. New York: Norton, 1991. A history of the wartime allies from 1933–1945 through the lenses of their leaders that emphasizes the accomplishments of their alliance rather than its failures.

Ellis, Joseph. *Founding Brothers: The Revolutionary Generation*. New York: Knopf, 2000. A Pulitzer Prize–winning history that explores the personalities of, and clashes between, such major figures as Washington, Adams, Burr, Hamilton, Jefferson, and Madison.

Fukuyama, Francis. *The End of History and the Last Man*. New York: Free Press, 1992. An influential and optimistic commentary on the post–Cold War future.

Gaddis, John Lewis. *Strategies of Containment: A Critical Appraisal of Postwar American National Security Policy during the Cold War*. Rev. and expanded ed. New York: Oxford University Press, 2005. An exceptionally valuable study that analyzes the specific and different Cold War containment strategies pursued by different presidential administrations.

———. *The United States and the Origins of the Cold War, 1941–1947.* New ed. New York: Columbia University Press, 2000. First published in 1972, this important post-revisionist volume focuses on the wartime and postwar origins of Soviet-American conflict and emphasizes the domestic constraints under which U.S. leaders labored.

———. *We Now Know: Rethinking Cold War History.* New York: Oxford University Press, 1997. This post–Cold War history of the conflict from its beginnings through the Cuban Missile Crisis makes use of newly available sources and emphasizes the differences between the U.S. and Soviet empires.

Gilbert, Felix. *To the Farewell Address: Ideas of Early American Foreign Policy.* Princeton, NJ: Princeton University Press, 1961. This major interpretation traces the idealistic and realistic strands in American foreign policy from their European and colonial roots to Washington's famous 1796 address.

Gilderhus, Mark T. *Pan-American Visions: Woodrow Wilson in the Western Hemisphere, 1913–1921.* Tucson, AZ: University of Arizona Press, 1986. This volume analyzes and criticizes Wilson's efforts to promote hemispheric integration under U.S. leadership and supervision.

Graebner, Norman A. *Foundations of American Foreign Policy: A Realist Appraisal from Franklin to McKinley* and *America as a World Power: A Realist Appraisal from Wilson to Reagan.* Wilmington, DE: Scholarly Resources, 1985. A compilation of essays on key events and policymakers from a realist perspective by one of the senior historians of U.S. foreign relations.

Greenstein, Fred I. *The Hidden-Hand Presidency: Eisenhower as Leader.* New York: Basic Books, 1982. (Johns Hopkins University Press 1994 reprint). An important and influential work in the positive reassessment of the Eisenhower presidency.

Gregory, Ross. *The Origins of American Intervention in the First World War.* New York: Norton, 1971. A brief and useful introduction to the factors that led to U.S. entry into the war.

Haliday, Jon, and Bruce Cumings. *Korea: The Unknown War.* New York: Pantheon Books, 1989. This revisionist account emphasizes the internal Korean origins of the war.

Harper, John Lamberton. *American Machiavelli: Alexander Hamilton and the Origins of U.S. Foreign Policy.* New York: Cambridge University Press, 2004. A recent and major reinterpretation of Hamilton's pivotal role in the making of early U.S. foreign policy.

Healy, David. *Drive to Hegemony: The United States in the Caribbean, 1898–1917.* Madison, WI: University of Wisconsin Press, 1988. An analysis of the techniques the United States developed for informal control over Caribbean nations, as well as the reasons it desired such control.

Heinrichs, Waldo. *Threshold of War: Franklin D. Roosevelt and American Entry into World War II.* New York: Oxford University Press, 1988. This analysis of Roosevelt's behavior in 1941 holds that FDR pursued a purposeful world strategy.

Herring, George C. *America's Longest War: The United States and Vietnam, 1950–1975.* 4th ed. New York: McGraw-Hill, 2002. Comprehensive and readable, this is one of the best overviews of the diplomatic and military history of the war. It emphasizes the Cold War context of the war and contains a useful bibliographic essay.

Higgins, Trumbull. *The Perfect Failure: Kennedy, Eisenhower and the CIA at the Bay of Pigs.* New York: Norton, 1987. A concise analysis of the numerous factors and individuals responsible for this U.S. failure.

Hoff, Joan. *American Business and Foreign Policy, 1920–1933.* Lexington, KY: University Press of Kentucky, 1971. The author uses the concept of "independent internationalism" to explain U.S. foreign policies during this era and to challenge the traditional "isolationist" label.

Hogan, Michael J., ed. *America in the World: The Historiography of American Foreign Relations Since 1941* and *Paths to Power: The Historiography of American Foreign Relations to 1900.* New York: Cambridge University Press, 1995, 2000. These volumes contain a series of useful historiographical essays on different time periods and issues in the history of U.S. foreign relations.

———, ed. *The End of the Cold War: Its Meaning and Implications.* New York: Cambridge University Press, 1992. An extensive collection of essays by major Cold War historians.

Hogan, Michael J., and Thomas G. Paterson, eds. *Explaining the History of American Foreign Relations.* 2nd ed. New York:

Cambridge University Press, 2004. A comprehensive and important collection of essays on the many different approaches to the study of American foreign relations used by contemporary historians.

Horsman, Reginald. *The Causes of the War of 1812*. Philadelphia, PA: University of Pennsylvania Press, 1962. The author examines the role of problems with Native Americans and Canada, as well as neutral rights on the high seas, in the coming of war in 1812.

————. *The Diplomacy of the New Republic, 1776–1815*. Arlington Heights, IL: Harlan Davidson, 1985. An excellent, brief introduction to the material covered in the first six lectures of this course, with a valuable bibliographic essay for those interested in additional readings.

————. *Race and Manifest Destiny: The Origins of American Racial Anglo-Saxonism*. Cambridge, MA: Harvard University Press, 1981. This major analysis and reinterpretation argues that "scientific" racism developed and played a major role in U.S. expansion in the first half and the end of the 19th century and that it resulted from a complex and mutually reinforcing interaction between European thought and American practice.

Hunt, Michael H. *Lyndon Johnson's War: America's Cold War Crusade in Vietnam, 1945–1968*. New York: Hill and Wang, 1996. A concise survey that emphasizes the role of cultural arrogance, as well as the Cold War.

Huntington, Samuel P. *The Clash of Civilizations and the Remaking of World Order*. New York: Simon and Schuster, 1996. A pessimistic view of the post–Cold War world that stands in stark contrast to the optimism of Fukuyama and others in the aftermath of Soviet collapse.

Isaacson, Walter. *Kissinger: A Biography*. New York: Simon and Schuster, 1992. One of the numerous good biographies of this key figure in the history of U.S. foreign policy during the Cold War era.

Jentleson, Bruce W., and Thomas G. Paterson, eds. *Encyclopedia of U.S. Foreign Relations*. 3 vols. New York: Scribner, 1984. A valuable reference work in the field; the three volumes contain 1,000 entries and suggestions for further reading prepared by specialists.

Jones, Howard. *Union in Peril: The Crisis over British Intervention in the Civil War*. Chapel Hill, NC: University of North Carolina Press, 1992. The author challenges the traditional view of Antietam and the Emancipation Proclamation ending the possibility of British intervention in the Civil War.

Kagan, Robert. *Dangerous Nation*. New York: Alfred A. Knopf, 2006. The first of two projected volumes reinterpreting American foreign policy from its beginnings through 1898 from a standpoint that challenges Americans' traditional image of themselves and emphasizes the degree to which others viewed the nation as highly aggressive and dangerous.

Kaplan, Lawrence S. *Colonies into Nation: American Diplomacy, 1763–1801*. New York: Macmillan, 1972. An important synthesis of material covered in the first four lectures of this course.

———. *Thomas Jefferson: Westward the Course of Empire*. Wilmington, DE: SR Books, 1999. This brief volume by a noted scholar of Jefferson and early U.S. foreign policy focuses on his support for westward expansion as a means of creating an "empire of liberty" free from the European powers.

Karnow, Stanley. *Vietnam: A History*. 2nd ed., rev. and updated. New York: Penguin Books, 1997. Originally published in 1983 as a companion to the acclaimed PBS television history of the war.

Kennan, George F. *American Diplomacy, 1900–1950*. Expanded ed. Chicago: University of Chicago Press, 1984. Originally published in 1951, this volume by one of the most notable Cold War–era officials and historians remains one of the most influential essays in the field. See also his highly regarded two-volume *Memoirs* (Boston: Little, Brown, 1967–1972).

Kennedy, Paul. *The Rise and Fall of the Great Powers: Economic Change and Military Conflict from 1500 to 2000*. New York: Random House. This bestselling interpretive history posits a strong relationship between economic growth and the rise to great-power status, on the one hand, and rapid fall from that status as a result of military overextension amidst relative economic decline, on the other.

Kimball, Warren F. *Forged in War: Roosevelt, Churchill, and the Second World War*. New York: William Morrow, 1997. A comprehensive and nuanced study of this vital wartime relationship written by the editor of the complete Churchill-Roosevelt correspondence.

Kissinger, Henry. *Diplomacy*. New York: Simon and Schuster, 1994. This broad survey of diplomatic history by a major Cold War policymaker and realist scholar emphasizes America's lack of appreciation for the European balance-of-power system. See also his massive, insightful, and controversial memoirs: *White House Years* (Boston: Little Brown, 1979); *Years of Upheaval* (Boston: Little, Brown, 1982); and *Years of Renewal* (New York: Simon and Schuster, 1999).

Kohn, Richard. *Eagle and Sword: The Federalists and the Creation of the Military Establishment in America, 1783–1802*. New York: Free Press, 1975. A detailed study of the politics of establishing both an armed force and a military policy for the infant United States.

LaFeber, Walter. *America, Russia, and the Cold War, 1945–2006*. 10th ed. New York: McGraw-Hill, 2008. A valuable interpretive and up-to-date survey of Russian-American relations during and after the Cold War years.

———. *Inevitable Revolutions: The United States in Central America*. 2nd ed. New York: W.W. Norton, 1993. First published in 1983 amidst a series of crises and interventions in Central America, this interpretive history argues that American policies in the area have led to the very revolutionary instability feared by the United States.

———. *The New Empire: An Interpretation of American Expansion, 1860–1898*. Rev. ed. Ithaca, NY: Cornell University Press, 1998. Originally published in 1963, this prize-winning analysis traces the roots of U.S. overseas imperialism to a major reassessment in the late 19th century that focused on the need for overseas expansion to resolve internal problems caused by industrialization.

Leffler, Melvyn P. *A Preponderance of Power: National Security, the Truman Administration, and the Cold War*. Stanford, CA: Stanford University Press, 1992. One of the most important works on the origins of the Cold War, this prodigiously researched and extensive volume analyzes the expansive ideological and geopolitical definitions of national security used by the Truman administration to explain U.S. policies during the early years of the Cold War.

Levin, N. Gordon. *Woodrow Wilson and World Politics: America's Response to War and Revolution*. New York: Oxford University Press, 1968. This important interpretive work views Wilson as a Lockean who championed liberal capitalist internationalism over both traditional Hobbesian imperialism and power politics, on one hand, and socialist revolution, on the other.

Lewis, Bernard. *What Went Wrong? The Clash between Islam and Modernity in the Middle East.* New York: Oxford University Press, 2002. A deeply influential work in the aftermath of 9/11 by a major Western historian of the Islamic world.

Lewis, James E., Jr. *John Quincy Adams: Policymaker for the Union.* Wilmington, DE: SR Books, 2001. This brief and recent biography emphasizes Adams's failures, along with his more recognized and numerous successes.

Link, Arthur S. *Woodrow Wilson: Revolution, War, and Peace.* Arlington Heights, IL: Harlan Davidson, 1979. This is a brief and useful introduction to Wilson's foreign policies—and to the conclusions of his foremost biographer and defender. For more extensive coverage, see Link's 5-volume biography *Wilson* (Princeton, NJ: Princeton University Press, 1947–1965) and 69-volume *The Papers of Woodrow Wilson* (Princeton, NJ: Princeton University Press, 1966–1994).

MacMillan, Margaret. *Paris 1919: Six Months That Changed the World.* New York: Random House, 2001. This award-winning, bestselling work is the first full-scale treatment of the Paris Peace Conference in more than 25 years.

Marks, Frederick. *Independence on Trial: Foreign Affairs and the Making of the Constitution.* 2nd ed. Wilmington, DE: Scholarly Resources, 1986. This is the only diplomatic survey of the Confederation era. The author maintains that concerns over foreign affairs were important factors in the demands for, and the creation of, a new frame of government.

May, Ernest. *The World War and American Isolation, 1914–1917.* Cambridge, MA: Harvard University Press, 1959. This detailed study analyzes British, German, and U.S. decision-making to explain how and why the United States entered World War I.

May, Robert E. *The Southern Dream of a Caribbean Empire, 1854–1861.* Baton Rouge, LA: Louisiana State University Press, 1973 (University Press of Florida 2002 reprint). An analysis of southern efforts to maintain Manifest Destiny expansion in the Caribbean and Central America during the 1850s.

Mayer, Arno. *Politics and Diplomacy of Peacemaking: Containment and Counterrevolution at Versailles, 1918–1919.* New York: Alfred A. Knopf, 1967. A major revisionist work that finds Allied leaders at least as concerned with containing Bolshevism in the aftermath of the Russian Revolution as they were with Germany

McCormick, Thomas J. *China Market: America's Quest for Informal Empire, 1893–1901.* Chicago: Quadrangle Books, 1967. Emphasizes the desire and perceived need for the China market as the focal point of American overseas expansion.

McDougall, Walter A. *Promised Land, Crusader State: The American Encounter with the World Since 1776.* Boston: Houghton Mifflin, 1997. This interpretive survey of U.S. foreign relations praises 18th- and 19th-century policymakers for their vision of an important but limited American role in the world but critiques their 20th-century successors for abandoning that vision in favor of an excessive crusading one.

Melanson, Richard A., and David Mayers, eds. *Reevaluating Eisenhower: American Foreign Policy in the 1950s.* Urbana, IL: University of Illinois Press, 1987. A major collection of essays in the 1980s reassessment of Eisenhower on some of his specific foreign policies.

Merrill, Dennis, and Thomas G. Paterson, eds. *Major Problems in American Foreign Relations.* 6th ed., 2 vols. Boston: Houghton Mifflin, 2005. These volumes contain excerpts from key documents and conflicting historical interpretations for a series of major issues in the history of U.S. foreign relations, ranging from the origins of American foreign policy through 9/11.

Morris, Richard B. *The Forging of the Union, 1781–1789.* New York: Harper and Row, 1987. This overview of the entire Confederation era fully covers the impact of foreign affairs on the movement for a stronger national government.

Onuf, Peter S. *Jefferson's Empire: The Language of American Nationhood.* Charlottesville, VA: University of Virginia Press, 2000. A detailed and provocative examination of Jefferson's vision of a republican empire and its numerous consequences.

Owsley, Frank L. *King Cotton Diplomacy: Foreign Relations of the Confederate States of America.* 2nd rev. ed by Harriet Chappell Owsley. Chicago: University of Chicago Press, 1959. First published in 1931, this volume remains a basic source on Confederate diplomacy during the Civil War.

Paterson, Thomas G. *On Every Front: The Making and Unmaking of the Cold War.* Rev. ed. New York: Norton, 1992. This interpretive history focuses on the structure of the post–World War II international system, the objectives and ideologies of the two powers, and the tactics and methods of their leaders.

———, ed. *Kennedy's Quest for Victory: American Foreign Policy, 1961–1963*. New York: Oxford University Press, 1989. A collection of essays sharply critical of Kennedy for his confrontational policies around the world.

Paterson, Thomas G., J. Garry Clifford, Shane J. Maddock, Deborah Kisatsky, and Kenneth J. Hagan. *American Foreign Relations: A History*. 6th ed., 2 vols. Boston: Houghton Mifflin, 2005. A highly readable, popular, and up-to-date textbook in the field.

Pletcher, David M. *The Diplomacy of Annexation: Texas, Oregon, and the Mexican War*. Columbia, MO: University of Missouri Press, 1973. A detailed study that criticizes James K. Polk for his aggressive diplomacy.

Reynolds, David. *From Munich to Pearl Harbor: Roosevelt's America and the Origins of the Second World War*. Chicago: Ivan R. Dee, 2001. An excellent overview of U.S. entry into World War II. See also his earlier *The Creation of the Anglo-American Alliance, 1937–1941: A Study in Competitive Cooperation* (Chapel Hill, NC: University of North Carolina Press, 1982).

Reynolds, David, Warren F. Kimball, and A. O. Chubarian, eds. *Allies at War: The Soviet, American, and British Experience, 1939–1945*. New York: St. Martin's Press, 1994. This collection of 16 essays by historians in all three countries covers military strategy, economics, the home front, and foreign policy for each country individually and for all three as allies.

Russett, Bruce M. *No Clear and Present Danger: A Skeptical View of United States Entry into World War II*. Rev. ed. New York: Harper and Row, 1972 (Westview Press 1997 reprint). This brief and provocative work maintains that Germany and Japan did not threaten U.S. security and that war with both powers could and should have been avoided.

Savelle, Max, with Margaret Anne Fisher. *The Origins of American Diplomacy: The International History of Angloamerica, 1492–1763*. New York: Macmillan, 1967. This volume looks to European diplomacy vis-à-vis the American mainland and Caribbean, as well as intercolonial relations, to explain the origins of American diplomacy.

Schulzinger, Robert D. *A Time for War: The United States and Vietnam, 1941–1975*. New York: Oxford University Press, 1997. A comprehensive and well-researched history that analyzes numerous aspects of the U.S. involvement in Vietnam.

Sheehan, Neil. *A Bright Shining Lie: John Paul Vann and America in Vietnam*. New York: Random House, 1988. A Pulitzer Prize–winning work that is part history and part journalist's memoir, as well as a biography of one of the most fascinating figures in the U.S. military effort in Vietnam.

Smith, Gaddis. *American Diplomacy during the Second World War, 1941–1945*. 2nd ed. New York: McGraw-Hill, 1985. This succinct survey offers a comprehensive overview of U.S. wartime diplomacy.

———. *Morality, Reason, and Power: American Diplomacy in the Carter Years*. New York: Hill and Wang, 1986. A balanced assessment of Carter's foreign policy successes and failures.

Spanier, John W. *The Truman-MacArthur Controversy and the Korean War*. Cambridge, MA: Belknap Press, 1959. This analysis locates the controversy in the nature of limited war and MacArthur's behavior and supports Truman's decision to relieve the general.

Stagg, J. C. A. *Mr. Madison's War: Politics, Diplomacy, and Warfare in the Early American Republic, 1783–1830*. Princeton, NJ: Princeton University Press, 1983. A comprehensive and important account of the political, diplomatic, and military history of the war.

Stephanson, Anders. *Manifest Destiny: American Expansionism and the Empire of Right*. New York: Hill and Wang, 1995. This brief volume focuses on the cultural underpinnings of American expansionism throughout U.S. history, with particular emphasis on religious concepts of American exceptionalism and mission.

Stueck, William W., Jr. *The Korean War: An International History*. Princeton, NJ: Princeton University Press, 1995. This comprehensive account emphasizes the international rather than the domestic Korean roots of the conflict.

Suri, Jeremi. *Power and Protest: Global Revolution and the Rise of Détente*. Cambridge, MA: Harvard University Press, 2003. This award-winning book sees détente as a conservative reaction to the global protests and disruptions of the late 1960s.

Tucker, Robert C., and David C. Hendrickson. *Empire of Liberty: The Statecraft of Thomas Jefferson*. New York: Oxford University

Press, 1990. This detailed study is highly critical of Jefferson's foreign policy ideas and record.

U.S. Department of State. *Foreign Relations of the United States.* Washington, DC: U.S. Government Printing Office, 1861– . This ongoing series, now numbering hundreds of volumes, constitutes the most comprehensive and important published source for official U.S. foreign policy documents.

Varg, Paul A. *Foreign Policies of the Founding Fathers.* East Lansing, MI: Michigan State University Press, 1964. This volume explores the idealistic and realistic strands in early American foreign policy, with Jefferson and Madison cast as the idealists and Hamilton as the realist.

Watts, Steven. *The Republic Reborn: War and the Making of Liberal America, 1790–1820.* Baltimore, MD: Johns Hopkins University Press, 1987. This reinterpretation emphasizes the war as playing an important role in the transition of the United States from the republican worldview of the Founding Fathers to the liberal capitalist worldview of the next generation.

Weeks, William Earl. *Building the Continental Empire: American Expansion from the Revolution to the Civil War.* Chicago: Ivan R. Dee, 1996. This brief interpretive survey focuses on the era of Manifest Destiny and sees a consensus on territorial and commercial empire as central to the construction and development of the nation until the 1850s.

———. *John Quincy Adams and American Global Empire.* Lexington, KY: University of Kentucky Press, 1992. The author sees Adams as a key individual in the American pursuit of global empire, with particular emphasis on the Transcontinental Treaty with Spain.

Westad, Odd Arne. *The Global Cold War: Third World Interventions and the Making of Our Times.* New York: Cambridge University Press, 2005. This prize-winning recent work sees the origins of contemporary international problems in the preceding extension of the Cold War into the third world.

Williams, William Appleman. *The Tragedy of American Diplomacy.* 2nd rev. and enl. ed. New York: Dell, 1972 (Norton 1988 reprint). This early and extraordinarily influential revisionist analysis sees 20th-century U.S. foreign policy as dominated by a belief that overseas economic expansion (as expressed in the Open Door policy) was necessary for domestic well-being—a belief that subverted American ideals and led to the creation of an informal global empire.

Yergin, Daniel. *Shattered Peace: The Origins of the Cold War*. Rev. and updated ed. New York: Penguin Books, 1990. Originally published in 1977, this influential work first posited the existence of two conflicting American perceptions of the Soviet Union— traditional great power with which one could work versus revolutionary state with which one could not—and the triumph of the latter as key to the ensuing Cold War.

Zubok, Vladislav M., and Constantine Pleshakov. *Inside the Kremlin's Cold War: From Stalin to Krushchev*. Cambridge, MA: Harvard University Press, 1996. Making use of recently released Soviet documents, two Russian historians reinterpret Soviet foreign policy based on Stalin's fusion of ideology and power politics.

CD 973 STOL
Stoler, Mark A.
 America and the World
Part 1 of 2
 (6 CDs + GUIDEBOOK)